The

Black Eyed

Children

2ND EDITION

by David Weatherly

EERIE LIGHTS PUBLISHING

The Black Eyed Children

2ND EDITION

**Based on interviews and research
conducted by David Weatherly**

Cover by: Sam Shearon
www.mister-sam.com

Editor: A. Dale Triplett
@DaleTriplett

Layout: SMAK
www.smakgraphics.com

ISBN 978-1-945950-04-9 (Paperback)

EERIE LIGHTS
EERIE LIGHTS PUBLISHING
Nevada

Black Eyes

Do not trust black eyes, but fear them:-

Gloom they are, and endless night;

Woes and perils lurking near them

Love not thou their gleaming bright!

From Avetis Isahakian
in *"Armenian Legends and Poems"*

Table of Contents

PART 1
The Black Eyed Children
Encounters and Legends

PART 2
The Theories

PART 3
Beyond The Children
Black Eyed Entities

Acknowledgements

This book is the result of countless interviews, fieldwork, hours of research and writing, and a lot of coffee.

As with any project like this, without the inspirations and behind the scenes support it would never have been completed. Ultimately, the love, help and support of countless friends and family members helped see this project through.

First and foremost, I want to thank my wife and kids for their patience and support during my countless hours of investigating the strange and unusual. You are my inspiration and I love you all deeply.

There is, of course, a long list of people who were early inspirations and helped put me on a path to explore the weird. They include John Keel, Jacques Vallee, Hans Holzer, Charles Fort, Erich Von Daniken and Ed and Lorraine Warren.

My endless hours as a kid sequestered away reading Fate magazine and watching shows such as 'In Search Of' fueled my interest in the strange. Because of my lifelong pursuits, I've been fortunate to find many kindred spirits along the way.

A special thanks to my friend and contemporary, Nick Redfern who helped encourage me during the writing of this book.

Thanks to all the radio programs and podcasts that interviewed me during my research of the black eyed children. Many of those interviews produced interesting new witnesses to the phenomenon and added more pieces to the unfolding puzzle.

My greatest thanks go out to all those who shared their stories of encounters with the black eyed kids. It takes a great deal of courage to share such intense, personal stories, especially with a stranger. This book wouldn't have been possible without you. I hope that you all find the peace you seek.

It's been a long road getting this material out. If I've missed anyone by name, trust me, it's not an intentional slight.

I hope you all enjoy this journey into the strange world of the black eyed children.

Foreword
by Nick Redfern

Just occasionally, a book comes along that I don't just recommend to people. Sometimes, I tell them they have to get a copy of it, no matter what! And that's the case with David Weatherly's, *The Black Eyed Children*, which is penned in masterful style.

There can be very few people interested in the realms of the paranormal, Fortean and Ufological who have not at least heard of the phenomenon, but if you haven't, well, David starts his book with the following, atmospheric words to get you acquainted with the admittedly creepy controversy:

"They just want to come inside. Across the world, there are a growing number of accounts of strange, black eyed children. They appear on doorsteps, at car windows, hotel rooms and even boats. Their skin is pale, their mannerisms odd and they have one consistent request. They want to be invited inside. What exactly is this growing phenomenon? Are they demonic entities? Alien hybrids? Perhaps they are some form of spirit seeking passage to another place. Or, are they simply a modern urban legend born of the computer age."

And it's these questions, and many others, that David addresses at length in the book you are now about to read.

What I particularly enjoyed about *The Black Eyed Children* - and one of the reasons why I feel the book is a profoundly important contribution to the BEC controversy - is that David not only relates the facts, the history, the rumors, the legends and theories relative to these kids, but he does so in a highly entertaining style. There's nothing worse than reading a book that is packed with data, but that is as dull as dishwater. Fortunately, David's book is anything but dull!

I don't exaggerate when I say that, in my opinion, this book is destined to become the definitive study on the puzzle, and for several reasons. Thankfully, and very refreshingly, David details the various scenarios that have been presented to explain the mystery, but he doesn't force-feed any particular one down the throat of his audience.

Rather, he presents the witness testimony, the case-files, and the supporting data and evidence, and then uses all of this as a springboard to try to determine which theory – or, indeed, theories – might be the correct one when it comes to trying to understand what these "things" are or are not. And, given the macabre nature of some of them, I'm perfectly satisfied in calling them "things." And after reading David's book, you may very well, too!

The book begins with a number of significant witness reports of encounters that are downright creepy. Yep, I know I used that word – creepy – earlier, but it really is the best way to describe these "Damien-meets-E.T." type kids.

A lot of people view the Black Eyed Children from that torturous "Love and Light" angle and perspective. You know the one: E.T. is dabbling with our DNA and creating half-human/half-alien kids that are super-intelligent and will play a big, positive role in our future as a species.

Well, David most certainly addresses, at length, the "hybrid" angle. But for me, I still get the deep feeling after reading his words that the phenomenon is very much self-serving and has its – rather than our – best interests at heart. And that's probably a black heart, too. You'll soon see what I mean as you delve deep into the book's pages.

This becomes particularly apparent when David begins to address such highly alternative areas relative to not just the far more conventional 'nuts and bolts'-UFO angle, but such realms as demonology; life after death and malevolent, tortured ghosts; Middle Eastern Djinn; definitive Tricksters; and a whole host of other entities that may not exactly be our best buddies in the slightest.

And, I'm pleased to say, David – always balanced and unbiased –

doesn't shy away from addressing the possibility that the whole thing is down to nothing stranger than modern-day urban legend. But, as he makes clear, even if some cases fall into that category, there is still a larger and wider mystery to be resolved. Like any aspect of Forteana, yes there are legends, hoaxes and friend-of-a-friend tales, but, strip them away and there's still a phenomenon – and that applies to the Black Eyed Children, too.

There's also an excellent chapter on the way in which certain medical conditions can affect the colors of the human eye – thus demonstrating that David leaves no stone unturned in his quest for the truth.

For me, the most fascinating sections of the book are those that highlighted the undeniable parallels between these eerie kids and the Men in Black, vampires and a host of other historical and horrific things that seem to take so much pleasure in tormenting us with their own, unique brands of evil mischief. Indeed, as you'll come to learn and appreciate the BEC seem to straddle the realms of many and assorted supernatural creatures.

As David notes, that the BEC reportedly, and specifically, have to be invited into the home of the person in their sights does, of course, evoke imagery of the classic bloodsuckers of Eastern Europe and elsewhere. And, with regard to the Men in Black, David says, intriguingly: "Perhaps the classic image of the MIB became too tame for some situations and a higher force created the black eyed children in order to grab the attention of a jaded, overwhelmed public that is tired of old stereotypes."

If your main area of interest when it comes to the paranormal is UFOs and aliens, then you are going to love this book. But, by delving deep into the hearts of a host of other supernatural conundrums too, *The Black Eyed Children* will also satisfy, intrigue and inform the student of demonology, mythology, ghosts and specters, succubi, and the age-old phenomenon of changelings, which is so prevalent in fairy-lore.

David Weatherly's *The Black Eyed Children* is a fascinating, insightful and remarkable piece of work on a subject that has been crying out for a definitive study - and now we have that definitive study. If you thought you knew all there was to learn about these strange characters, you're about to get a big wake-up call! Maybe a literal wake-up call, too, if 'they' come knocking on your door on some dark, chilled night as the witching-hour looms large.

Read, appreciate, enjoy, and keep a careful look over your shoulder. You know: just in case...

Nick Redfern is the author of many books, including *Monster Diary; The Real Men in Black; and Wild Man.*

Introduction

They just want to come inside.

Across the world, there are a growing number of accounts of strange, black eyed children. They appear on doorsteps, at car windows, hotel rooms, and even near docked boats. Their skin is pale, their mannerisms odd, and they have one consistent request.

They want to be invited inside.

What exactly is this growing phenomenon? Are they demonic entities? Alien hybrids? Some form of spirit seeking passage to another place? Or are they simply a modern urban legend born of the computer age?

When I first heard tales of the black-eyed kids, or 'BEKs' as they are sometimes called, I thought the phenomenon could likely be explained easily. Perhaps the stories were simply the result of someone with too many hours to waste behind a keyboard. Maybe there was a prankster who donned black contacts and decided to make a name for himself in the field of urban legends.

My opinion changed, however, when I began to hear personal accounts from people who had encountered these strange children. These people had run into something that terrified them, and there were many, many unanswered questions in the wake of the encounters.

These were normal, upstanding people. Among them were

police officers, firefighters, military personnel, doctors, nurses and other, everyday people. They were not seeking publicity. Indeed, the greater portion of them refused to have their stories told, even with the promise of anonymity. They simply wanted to understand what they had encountered.

In the following pages, you will find some of the stories gathered over the course of several years of exploring the phenomenon of the black eyed kids. For the privacy of those who have shared their experiences, I have used only first names in the accounts.

There seems little doubt that confronting these beings is a life-altering event for most people. A common theme among those I interviewed, is that after their disturbing experience, they turned to more spiritual pursuits and lifestyles, seeking something that would give them comfort and possible protection in the event the children returned into their lives.

There are obvious difficulties when investigating phenomena such as this. No black eyed kid has ever been cornered or captured. I have not discovered any genuine photographs or video footage. Indeed, photographs would be practically useless in this day and age since the "black eyed" effect is an easy thing to create digitally. On the few occasions surveillance cameras have been present during these encounters, they mysteriously stopped working or experienced 'glitches' that caused them to skip time and record nothing during the incident.

What we do have are stunning accounts. Stories about experiences that were life changing. These accounts come from people from all walks of life. They are both personal, and at times, disturbing.

I hope by presenting the information I have gathered here we can move closer to understanding what this phenomenon means and why it seems to be spreading.

Introduction
to the Second Edition

It's hard to believe it's been five years since the first publication of The Black Eyed Children. In that time, accounts have continued to pour in from all corners of the globe. Numerous researchers have joined the fray and have gathered reports and firsthand accounts. Theories have been expanded, more details and data have been collected, and through it all, one thing has remained consistent:

The children still want to come inside.

It seems I'm often noted as the go to expert on the BEK phenomena, this came about because I was the first to publish a complete study on the topic. However, I always try to give credit where it's due and I like to point out, that while I was the first to publish a book completely devoted to the topic, I was not the first to write about the strange children. Notable explorers of the paranormal who wrote on the topic before include Jason Offutt and Brad Steiger. Additionally, radio programs such as Coast to Coast AM and Darkness Radio have long been taking accounts from listeners who have run into the BEKs.

When I first started investigating the subject of these encounters, one of my main goals was to find accounts that predated modern Internet tales of the BEKs. I was also hoping to find accounts that predated the use of solid black eyes as a special effect on television and in films.

I was indeed fortunate to find such early tales, and since the book's first release, many more accounts have been dug up by both myself and others doing research into the topic.

Key to finding these early accounts has been the removal of the common terms used in modern encounters; black eyed children, black eyed kids, and the acronym BEK. When we remove these terms, yet keep the same basic parameters of the encounters, many more accounts surface. Through various cultural and time-period lenses, we find there are accounts of black eyed entities far back through history.

An interesting note, is that Brian Bethel, the man whose personal encounter is famous for starting the modern wave of sightings, has stated to me that he wished he'd never come up with the term BEK. Bethel believes the term has somehow limited the exploration into what the black eyed entities actually are. This may be the case, at least to some degree, since there are still many people who believe this is a phenomenon of recent origin.

As more and more reports surface, it becomes clear we are dealing with a long history of encounters with black eyed beings and that, despite countless accounts, we still have no clear answer to explain exactly what we're dealing with.

Now, five years later, I'm pleased to release a revised edition of my original exploration into the strange children. As a writer, looking back on something written years ago, it's difficult to not be critical of one's own style at the time. I have however, resisted the urge to do a massive rewrite of the book. This new edition has been re-edited and slightly revised, streamlined if you will, to hopefully, make it even more reader friendly. All the primary information from the original edition is still here. New to this edition is a fascinating piece of commentary from Brian Bethel reflecting on his encounter and its aftermath.

I hope you enjoy this exploration into these strange, unexplained encounters.

David Weatherly
Somewhere in the Desert
2017

PART 1:
The Black Eyed Children
Encounters & Legends

Chapter I

Basic Black

It's been a long day at work.

You've just arrived home, put your things down and headed to the fridge. As you reach inside for a cold drink, you hear a sound.

It's a knock at the door.

It's not loud but it feels intrusive after a hard day. It's a steady knock, almost monotonous. *Why don't they use the doorbell?* you wonder as you head to the door.

You open it to find two children around twelve to fourteen years old.

They want to come in.

They want YOU to invite them in.

You have no idea who these kids are or why they want to enter your house. You've never seen them in the neighborhood. Not only that, but there's something else. You can't quite put your finger on it, but there's something that just seems wrong about these children. You feel dizzy; your head is in a fog.

They stand there on the steps as the sun is setting, repeating the same comments over and over.

"Why don't you just ask us in?"

"Tell us to come in so we can use the phone."

You know something's wrong. You feel like you should close the door, but you're frozen in place, unable to move in or out. You begin to wrestle with the choice before you. They are, after all, only children; they should be harmless and maybe they need help. What would happen if you let them inside? You realize you're sweating, shaking. You feel on the verge of panic and you feel foolish at the same time.

You look back at the children again and it's then you realize what's wrong with their appearance. Their eyes are black--solid black. You slam the door shut, moving quickly to your bedroom and closing that door too, hoping to feel safe.

Echoing in the quiet house, you hear a sound--a long constant knocking on the front door.

You've just encountered the black eyed children.

Traits of the BEKs

The accounts sound like something straight out of a horror movie.

It almost always begins with a knock. Sometimes it's a knock at the front door of your home; sometimes it's a gentle rap on the window of your car as you sit in a parking lot.

From nowhere, the children are there. Sometimes there's only one, often they are in pairs, on occasion there are more. They have a tale of distress, an expression of need, they need to use your phone, or the bathroom. Perhaps they need a ride or something to eat. They assure you, *"It won't take long."*

At first, they seem well mannered and polite—perhaps too polite. While the average child or teenager is not inclined to approach adults, these children have no qualms about doing so. There is no shyness on their part. In fact, they have no qualms when it comes to making their requests either.

They have come to be called 'black eyed children' or 'BEKs,' short for 'black eyed kids.' No one knows where these beings come from or exactly what they want. For that matter, no one knows exactly what they are. Although a large percentage of the accounts come from the United States, encounters have been documented from around the world. Locations as diverse as the UK, Australia, Canada, South Africa and Iraq have stories of the black eyed children.

A number of common traits inevitability show up in the accounts. First and foremost, of course, are the black eyes. This is not a case of children with dark pupils. In these cases, both the pupil and the sclera, or white of the eye, are solid black. Witnesses use terms such as 'shiny' or 'liquid' when noting the depth of the children's eyes.

"It's unnatural," said one witness. *"Those eyes are so black and they have a shine to them. I don't think anything human could have eyes like that."*

Most healthy humans have a white-colored sclera. The sclera is a very thin tissue that compromises 5/6 of the outer surface of the eye. Human eyes are filled with a clear gelatinous material. This material must be clear to permit the unobstructed passage of light from the lens to the retina of the eye. A human with a solid black pupil and sclera would be mostly blind because little to no light would be able to enter the eye.

As if solid black eyes were not disturbing enough, the children are often reported to have very pale skin. This, of course, causes the eyes to stand out even more. *"It* [the skin] *looked pasty to me,"* commented one man who encountered the kids. *"There was something wrong with his skin to be that white and pale. It gave him a gaunt appearance."* The skin color has led some people to speculate the kids are sick or at least malnourished.

Other witnesses described the skin as 'olive-toned' or unnaturally tinted in some way. One witness referred to it as *"like a spray on tan, but the wrong color."* She believed the BEKs had possibly applied makeup to hide their true skin color.

The next thing noted by witnesses is the clothing the children wear. It's described as 'ill fitting' or 'old fashioned.' One woman noted, *"It looked almost Amish or something. Maybe it was handmade, but it didn't fit right either. I guess they could have been wearing hand-me-down clothes."* This is one of the common interpretations of the attire - it's too large and looks baggy on the child, or it is ragged in appearance. The colors are almost always basic—dull whites, grays, brown and black.

In some cases, the children are wearing modern clothing, usually 'hoodies' and jeans. But even in these incidents, the clothing is nondescript and the colors remain basic dark shades. *"It's as though*

3

the kids are trying to blend in, but it just doesn't come off right," said one person.

A man in Ohio who encountered the BEKs thought perhaps they were homeless children. *"They looked grungy to me. I thought they had gotten those clothes from some shelter, or out of the garbage, because they didn't fit right. They also looked like they didn't eat much, but maybe that's because the clothes were so baggy. I've seen street children before."* He continued, *"The sad state of their clothes made me think about that."*

The ill-fitting clothing obscures the children's true size and adds to the difficulty witnesses have in determining how old the kids really are. As with the skin tone, the drab clothing also contributes to the unusual depth of the eyes.

Not only is the appearance and attire of the BEKs unusual, so is their use of language. It is described as formal and polite, but at the same time, awkward and strained. One witness reports, *"It's almost as if they were taught a couple of lines. They memorized them and just kept repeating the same things over and over. You know, like someone reading from a script. And some of the words, it's like they had practiced saying them. I just don't hear kids talk like that."*

Yet another person who encountered a black eyed child claimed the boy, *"sounded like he was programmed. I don't know how to describe it. It was overly proper but routine. Like the computer telling you that you have mail."*

Not only is their use of language strange; it usually contains odd requests that startle the witnesses:

"Just let us in; this won't take long."

"We'll just stay for a bit."

"We're only kids; don't worry about it."

"I'd never seen these kids before in my life," reports one person who found a pair of BEKs knocking at his front door.

"They wanted to come in and watch television. I was just stunned. I'd never have knocked on a stranger's door and asked such things when I was a child."

Witnesses find the strange requests disturbing but it doesn't stop there. The children are insistent that they "need" to come inside, as if they are running out of time for something. At times, their requests are tailored to the location. Witnesses who have been in vehicles when encountering the children find them asking for a ride.

"He told me he needed a ride and that he was only a kid," reports a woman who encountered a black eyed child at a gas station. *"He was just there before I could even get out to pump my gas. I started the car back up and drove away. It was just all too creepy."*

The black eyed kids have turned up at homes and apartments, hotel rooms, cars, even boats. Their requests become more demanding when the adults exhibit reluctance, as if pressing the adult will force them to stop hesitating and give in to the request.

The children also appear to believe they can lull people into following their directions if they keep repeating their requests over and over.

"They don't break their rhythm; nor do they respond if you ask them questions," reports John. He encountered a pair of black eyed children at his hotel room in Honolulu.

"I thought it was room service knocking at the door. I open it, and here's this pair of kids with black eyes. They wanted to come in and watch television with me. It was all rather absurd. I asked them why they didn't go to their own room. They wouldn't answer; they just kept repeating the same things. I wondered if it was all some kind of joke and I looked up and down the hallway. The one kid told me I should just let them in, that it wouldn't take long. I slammed the door on them at that point. I realized that I was shaking, I don't know why those kids made me so nervous."

Some people believe the children are attempting to exert a form of hypnosis or mind control. *"The speech is monotone and it sort of drones into you when you start to listen to it. They ignored everything I said to them and just kept repeating the same phrases,"* recalled Linda.

If the children are attempting hypnosis, it may explain why they refuse to respond to direct questions. One witness related his impression of a black eyed child's speech pattern, *"It had a hypnotic quality really. I felt compelled to just do what they were asking me to and even felt my body moving but at the same time there was some deep fear that kicked in. I felt like, if I did listen to this boy, this little boy, and if I did what he said then I might not be around anymore. Why should a kid scare me like that?"*

Ironically, it would appear this attempted hypnosis on the children's part causes the fight or flight response to kick in. More than one person has slammed the door, or turned and run away when encountering a BEK.

"I compare it to infrasound," says John. (Infrasound is low frequency sound beyond the normal limit of human hearing. It is used by some animals as a defense mechanism and causes a variety of reactions in the human nervous system).

"Afterwards I realized my body was shaking," John continued. *"My nerves were on edge and I felt like I just wanted to run as far away as I could as quick as I could."*

"My stomach was in knots," recalls Beth, a witness from Chicago. *"I was scared senseless. I can't understand how a pair of children could be so frightening. My logical mind kept telling me they were just kids and needed help, but I couldn't bear the fear reaction from my body."*

Beth also reported feeling a sense of dread when confronting the children. *"I felt like they were sizing me up,"* she said. *"It's almost like they were a pair of predators and they were deciding how to take me down. At the same time, they were trying to act so polite. The combination was nerve wracking."*

Beth is not alone in her sense of malevolent energy coming from the children. Numerous reports of BEK encounters contain words such as 'predatory,' 'sinister' and 'evil.'

Some people have a difficult time explaining their impression of this energy. *"It's not any one thing that they did,"* recalled one man. *"It was just this aura or something that scared the hell out of me. I couldn't make sense of it because on the surface it was just a young kid."*

Although they have been known to show up at any hour, the bulk of encounters with black eyed beings occur in the evening, often just as the sun is setting.

Another trait very common in BEK encounters is the seeming ability of the children to move quickly, silently, and, at times, disappear completely and suddenly. More than one witness has glanced away for just a moment, and when turning back to the children, found they had moved much closer.

"I glanced back in my door. Just a quick glance. When I turned back those kids were much closer to me. I didn't hear or see them move and I can't

imagine how they did so that quickly. It was like they could somehow just glide across the floor without making any sound."

No doubt this is an unnerving effect to experience. Other witnesses have turned away from the children for a moment, and when looking back find the kids have vanished completely.

"There wasn't anywhere for them to go. There was nothing to hide behind, nowhere to run to. They were just gone without a trace."

This bizarre ability has led to speculation that the children can fly, teleport, or move between dimensions. It's quite stunning to hear a trained police officer insist that children vanished from his field of vision in a matter of seconds, and that searches of the area revealed no trace of the kids ever having been present.

A portion of the accounts I have reviewed report another unnerving quality connected to the black eyed children—a foul, stomach-turning odor. This smell has been described as 'rotten eggs,' 'decaying garbage,' or 'rotting meat.' The smell is sometimes only noted after the children have disappeared from the area. It causes nausea and sometimes light-headedness. The unpleasant odor often lingers in the area for hours after the encounter.

There are other less common attributes associated with the BEKs. Some people have heard a strange scream with an animal-like quality. One witness swears the black eyed children multiplied when he briefly turned his head.

On rare occasions, video cameras have been present where an individual encountered the kids. Later review of the video tape or recordings showed no sign of the children. Recordings have been blank, glitches caused the tapes to skip forward, or the system was found to have been shut down entirely without any human agent being involved. On at least one occasion, a video tape showed the witness talking to thin air.

The black eyed children are difficult to classify. Since they are human, (at least in appearance) they do not fall in the realm of cryptids. Arguments abound as to their origins. With the increase of encounters and reports, numerous theories have been presented to explain what they are.

These theories include:

Aliens, Alien Hybrids or a version of the Men In Black

Demons or demonic entities

Some form of undead entity.

Ghosts or spirits

Of course, skeptics would like to believe all the encounters are hoaxes, kids playing pranks, or children with medical conditions.

Most people who encounter the BEKs are reluctant to talk about their experiences. The encounters are unsettling and difficult to forget. Witnesses are left wondering what the children wanted and what would have happened had they given in to the odd request. Some people are very traumatized by the experience, often refusing to return to the place of the encounter, or refusing to answer the door when friends or relatives visit. Those who have had close encounters with the BEKs are frequently plagued by bad dreams in the days and weeks following the experience.

"Those eyes, I just can't get them out of my mind," lamented one witness.

What is it about these strange children that is so unnerving? How are they able to unbalance even the sturdiest of personalities? Somehow they produce an unreasonable level of fear, and in some cases sheer panic. The fight or flight mechanism takes control and quickly becomes a pure flight response when the black eyed kids arrive.

Children, especially those that appear to be in need, tug at our innate emotions. It's easy for a child to provoke an adult's natural protective instinct. It's this sympathetic reaction that often catches people off guard when encountering the BEKs. The first reaction of most witnesses is that a child needs help; hence, the natural 'guard' and defenses come down.

Children in horror movies have a profound effect on the viewer. It's hard for the average adult mind to place a child in the role of something evil. When this occurs, the mind and emotions are pulled in opposite directions, trying to comprehend how something innocent (a child) could also be something dark and sinister. Perhaps this is why the black eyed children, whatever they are, appear in the form of young children.

Chapter 2

Brian Bethel
& the Modern Age of BEKs

Anyone, anywhere, who has an interest in the BEK phenomena has likely heard the name Brian Bethel. His story is by far the most often repeated, and most widely mentioned account concerning the weird children.

In fact, Bethel gained so much attention from his classic encounter it caused him to pull well away from the public eye for years. He attempted to put the case behind him, having grown tired of being asked the same questions about the children again and again.

It's only in recent years that Bethel has again become comfortable, to some degree, talking about his encounter with the BEKs. In a strange way, his long period of reluctance in discussing the incident added more credence to his story. While skeptics like to think people like Brian make up stories to get attention, it's clear in this case that massive attention was the last thing Bethel wanted. He simply wanted to understand what had happened, and maybe, gain some knowledge about what the "kids" he encountered actually were.

The Brian Bethel Story

The first modern, and I stress modern, documented case involving the black eyed children is the encounter reported by journalist Brian Bethel. The account was first posted on the Internet in 1998 and many people believe it's responsible for starting the trend of Internet BEK stories. Numerous black eyed kid accounts followed, but Bethel's story is often the first one recounted when anyone starts talking about the children.

When Bethel posted the story, he had no idea it would catch on the way it did. To him, it was just a weird encounter he chose to share online in hopes of some feedback. Something about the story resonated with people, and in the ensuing years, it found its way onto countless paranormal websites.

Bethel's encounter with the children occurred in Abilene, Texas. It was between nine thirty and ten o'clock at night. He had gone to pay a bill at a shopping center, intending to drop a check in an after-hours payment box. While sitting in his car writing out his check, he was startled by a knock on the driver's side window.

Bethel looked up and saw two boys. He estimated them to be between ten and fourteen years of age. They appeared average at first glance. Normal hair, normal build and normal clothes that were in style for the time. The first boy had an olive complexion and brown hair of medium length. The second boy was pale-skinned and had pale orange hair.

Initially, Bethel didn't notice anything unusual at all. He assumed the kids were going to ask for money or some other handout. As he had that thought, however, something changed.

Bethel recounts the moment: *"...right before I experience something strange, there's a change in perception that comes about...It's basically enough time to know it's too late."*

These aspects of Bethel's story are very similar to typical accounts of the BEKs. People experience an uneasy feeling that something is wrong, while everything seems normal on the surface. Bethel felt a sudden panic coming over him, but at the same time, a sense of confusion.

In Bethel's case, like many others, the solid dark eyes were not noticed right away. This is sometimes due to the children looking slightly down instead of making eye contact. Bethel's odd reaction seems to be based on a subtle energy coming from the boys. His car was still running and he felt his fight or flight response kicking in. As Bethel's encounter continued, he cracked his window slightly and asked the boys what they wanted. They told him they wanted to see a movie, but they had left their money at home. They requested that Brian "help them out" by taking them home to retrieve the cash.

Bethel was hesitant. Something about the boys, especially the speaker's smile, made him extremely nervous. His lack of response to the boys provoked further comments from the speaker.

"C'mon mister. Now, we just want to go to our house and we're just two little boys."

Again, this is standard behavior from the black eyed kids. They go out of their way to convince adults they are only kids, implying they are harmless and obviously in need of help. Bethel was composed enough to ask questions and to notice that, according to the movie marquee, the last show of the evening had already been playing for an hour. The boy pressed Bethel further, commenting

"C'mon mister, let us in. We can't get in your car until you let us you know. Just let us in and we'll be gone before you know it."

Again, we see the common theme of BEK encounters. The assurance of, "this won't take long" or "we'll be gone before you know it." It all seems very sinister when you consider the terms coupled with the energy emitted by the kids. At this point in his encounter, Bethel finally made eye contact with the boys.

"They were coal black, -no pupil, no Iris -s-just two staring orbs reflecting the red and white light of the marquee," he recalled.

Like many others who encounter the black eyed children, the sight of the eyes proved to be the final straw for Bethel. He raced away from the kids, stealing a quick look back as he did so, but the kids were nowhere in sight.

Bethel's account was originally posted on an Internet bulletin board, and his story prompted other people to tell of their own similar encounters with black eyed beings. While other accounts pre-date Bethel's story, his is the one that generated the most attention for a long time, setting the standard for others to come.

Urban Legends

I'd heard stories about the black eyed children from time to time in the late 1990's and into the early 2000's. Most of them were second or third-hand accounts with no clear indication of the actual location or people involved. Although the accounts were intriguing, on the surface, the BEKs sounded like another urban myth.

An urban legend or urban myth is a form of modern folklore. Urban legends consist of tales the storyteller may or may not believe to be factual. To further add to the confusion, urban legends are not always rooted in urban environments; rather, the term is used to distinguish more modern stories from older, traditional folktales.

Urban legends usually take the form of stories that happened to 'a friend of a friend.' Originally, they were the stories one would hear around schools and college campuses, around the water cooler at work, or at the local pub. With the advent of the Internet and social media, urban legends found a new breath of life. They are now circulated on forums, in chat rooms, on websites, and via email. While the root of the tale usually remains the same, details often shift about freely, depending on the person relating the story. Much like a game of telephone, the longer a story continues and grows, the more twists and turns the tale seems to take.

Jan Harold Brunvand, professor of English at the University of Utah has studied these urban tales extensively. He popularized the term 'urban Legend' when he published a series of books covering the most well-known tales. His titles, included *"The Choking Doberman"* and *"The Mexican Pet,"* and were popular best sellers in the early 1980's.

Brunvand believes much can be learned about modern culture and life in urban environments by studying contemporary urban legends and the way people react to the tales. Such tales usually contain a strong warning to the person listening to the story. After all, anyone could fall victim and find themselves in the middle of one of these terrifying situations.

The well-known tale of Bloody Mary is a popular example of these tales. Stand before a mirror in the darkness and repeat the name Bloody Mary three times, and she is reported to appear. While some believe the Bloody Mary game has roots in older lore, others believe it to be a complete fabrication. Fact or fantasy? It's one of those tales that falls squarely into the urban legend category.

Modern versions of urban legends incorporate contemporary concerns and fears. Theft of organs and other body parts, and violence linked to gang-related initiations are two themes currently making the rounds in modern urban legends.

Disbelievers are anxious to claim the entire black eyed children phenomenon was 'started' via the Internet and the first posted story by journalist Brian Bethel.

The primary difference between urban legends and accounts of the black eyed children, however, is it's easy to find people who have directly experienced encounters with the black eyed kids. Whereas urban legends are popular to tell, most of the people who have encounters with the BEKs are extremely reluctant to talk about the incidents.

Paul's Story

While I was curious about BEK reports, it wasn't until I spoke at length to a gentleman who'd encountered them himself that I became interested in further delving into the accounts.

I'd known Paul on a casual level for a couple of years. He knew about my interest in and pursuit of paranormal subjects, but it wasn't something he was personally interested in. He was one of those people who would occasionally ask questions or crack a joke. Although he constantly professed his disbelief, he couldn't seem to leave the topic alone. I've dealt with such people through the years, and I knew it was a matter of time before it was clear why Paul couldn't stop asking about supernatural topics.

Finally, I ran into him one day while I was having lunch. He asked if he could join me and we started talking in depth about various subjects. He broached the paranormal but not in his usual, joking way. While we were enjoying some coffee, Paul finally opened up and revealed his personal story. Like many people trying to find reason in something they couldn't understand, Paul prefaced his account with a statement about his disbelief.

"I want you to know that I just don't believe in Bigfoot or flying saucers or anything like that."

There was an unspoken 'but' hanging in the air. I've encountered this many times over the years. A 'nonbeliever' who, despite a skeptical attitude, has some experience they simply can't explain in rational terms.

"No problem Paul," I responded, *"If there's something you want to*

tell me about, go ahead; I won't judge you."

He shifted around a bit, clearly trying to get comfortable and focus. He wasn't the kind of person who was used to opening up and this was obviously difficult for him. Clearly though, it was something he needed to talk about.

"It's just something that happened and I've never been able to understand it. I figured with all the weird stuff you've researched maybe you've got some insight on it."

"I'll certainly give you any information I can," I replied.

Paul took a deep breath and sat back. When he began his story, a visible change came over him. Paul was not a small man. He stood around 6'3" and looked like a linebacker. I knew he lifted weights on a regular basis and actively trained in martial arts. He had been in the service when he was young, then worked for years as a prison guard. He was a man who had been in some very intense situations. In his time, he had seen brutal fights, prison brawls, knife attacks— the worst society had to offer. Nothing seems to have prepared him, however, for his run in with the black eyed children.

Paul was still working as a guard at a Midwest prison when he had his encounter. He arrived home from work one evening after a dayshift at the prison. He changed out of his uniform and went to the kitchen to prepare a sandwich. Since his wife and son were out of town for a few days, Paul had the house to himself. He decided to relax, have a couple of beers, and watch some sports before turning in for the night.

"Wasn't often that I had the house to myself," he said. *"I just wanted to enjoy a really low key, relaxing night."*

Standing in the kitchen, he heard a knock at the front door.

"At first, I wasn't even sure it was a knock," said Paul. *"It was kind of soft and continuous and I thought maybe it was just some other noise from outside. I kept making my food and ignored it for a few minutes. Then it got louder and I knew it must be someone knocking at the front door."*

It was odd, he thought, that the person didn't ring the doorbell. Paul left his food on the counter and approached the front door. He looked out of one of the small, side panel windows on the door's frame and saw two young boys on the porch. He guessed from their size they were between twelve and fourteen years old.

Paul opened the door and looked at the kids. They weren't children from his neighborhood because he knew all the local kids. The boys were dressed in similar fashion, both wearing hoodies and jeans. One boy's top was gray and the other boy's top was dark brown. The boy in brown stood slightly behind the boy in the gray hoodie and they both held their heads tilted downward, both silent and saying nothing.

"I thought something was odd about the scene and neither child said anything when I opened the door. They just stood there with their heads down, like you'd do in the rain, but it wasn't raining."

Paul broke the silence. *"Can I help you?"* he asked.

He expected a sales pitch; perhaps the kids were fund-raising for school or selling magazines. Maybe they just had the wrong house. What he didn't expect was the response he received.

The lead boy in gray kind of smiled and replied, *"Hey...we just wanted to stop in for a bit."*

Paul was puzzled by the odd reply. *"It's almost like I didn't understand the statement,"* he said. *"I knew these boys weren't friends of my son's because I knew my son's friends, and he was much younger than these two anyway."*

After a moment, Paul responded to the boys. *"Do I know you guys? I think maybe you've got the wrong house."*

The boys didn't react to Paul's comment. After a moment, the lead boy spoke again. *"Oh, well, it's getting kinda late...Can we come in for a bit?"*

It was another odd response and Paul wasn't sure what to think about the situation.

"Something was causing the hair on the back of my neck to go up," he recalled. *"I felt like this kid was ignoring me and focusing on me all at the same time. It just made no sense. Why in hell would a couple of kids show up at a stranger's door and want to come in?"*

With his internal alarms going off, Paul began to look at the kids even more closely. It was early evening and the porch light was on, so he shifted his stance to get a better look at their faces. He wanted to know exactly who these boys were and what they were up to. It was then that Paul realized with a shock that the boy's eyes were solid black. *"There was no white of the eye,"* he said.. *"I've thought about that sight ever since. They didn't have on any kind of glasses or anything else. That was their natural eyes that I saw."*

The lead boy looked up directly at Paul and spoke again. This time his voice was more insistent and he suddenly seemed more threatening.

"It would be good if you just let us come in now. You don't have to think about it. Just open the door some and ask us in."

Paul felt rooted to the spot; his brain was trying to process what was happening. *"I didn't feel like I could move, I was a little dizzy and had kind of a numb feeling. I started thinking that maybe I should just let them in; after all, they were only a couple of kids."*

Paul wasn't sure how long he stood there. He felt locked in the moment, trying to make his body move. The same boy spoke once more.

"It's okay; this won't take long."

"That comment jerked me into action," Paul stated. *"All of a sudden, I felt my fight or flight response kick in and it got me moving."*

Even though Paul towered over these two boys, his response was one of fear. He slammed the door shut, shouting at the boys to get off his porch as he did so.

"Last thing I saw as I was slamming the door shut was those two boys looking at me. Two sets of those creepy, solid black eyes just boring a hole in me."

With the door closed, Paul leaned against it. *"I felt like I had to hold it shut,"* he said. He locked the deadbolt and stood quietly trying to calm himself. His adrenaline was still rushing and he felt short of breath.

Then came the knock.

"It was a long, steady knock on the door. Soft at first, just like I had heard to begin with. Those damn boys still wanted in."

"I realized I'd been squeezing my eyes shut. I opened them and looked around the room. It's like I just didn't know what to do. I think I fought the urge to run at that point. My brain was telling me it was my house and I

wasn't running from kids but another part of me just wanted to hide."

Paul turned and slowly backed away from the front door. He stopped partway across the room and stood looking at the entrance to his home. The knocking stopped. Paul felt a cold chill come over him. There, staring in through the side panel window was the face of one of the boys, his black eyes looking into the living room, staring straight at Paul. They made eye contact and the boy raised a hand, tapping on the glass as he peered inside. Paul took a deep breath, feeling his anger rise.

"I'd had enough. No one was going to invade my home, or make me feel afraid like that. I ran into the bedroom and retrieved my pistol from the nightstand. I was determined to scare these punk kids off my property."

Paul put a clip in his gun and rushed back to the living room. He flung the front door wide open and stepped out on the porch, determined to face the strange kids.

They were nowhere in sight.

"It was the weirdest thing. The porch was empty but I know it had only taken me a couple of minutes at the most to grab and load that pistol. I searched the yard front and back, the driveway, garage, and I even went up and down the street. There was no sign of those black eyed boys anywhere."

Paul couldn't sleep that night. He kept thinking about the two strange kids who had shown up on his doorstep. He walked the house constantly, checking the doors and windows. The next day was his day off and he made it a point to speak to his neighbors to find out if any of them had seen the kids. No one else reported any sign of unusual boys or strange kids in the area.

"For a long time, I didn't tell anybody what I had seen. They'd think I was nuts. Heck, I thought maybe I was nuts at first. I know what I saw though. Weeks later, I was still thinking about it. I couldn't talk to my wife about it because I didn't want her to worry about anything, especially with a young child at home. I even asked a friend of mine who was a doctor if it was possible for someone to have solid black eyes. He just laughed and said no, that didn't happen. Finally, one day I decided to look on the Internet and I found a couple of stories. Turned out other people had seen black eyed kids before. I couldn't read that stuff though. It was enough to know that someone else had seen them and that I wasn't crazy, but at the same time, it disturbed me, because it sort of confirmed that these things were out there."

Paul sat back, finished with his story. I let him have a few moments to regain his composure. Obviously, relating the tale, even after so long, took a toll on him.

He also told me that over the years he had only related the story of his encounter to three other people. No one could give him any answers or solace, and even though it had been several years since the incident, he still felt haunted by it.

"It's those eyes. I've never been able to really get them out of my head."

Paul felt plagued by questions he couldn't answer regarding the children who appeared at his door that night. What did they really want? How had they vanished so quickly? What would have happened if he let them in, and most importantly for Paul, how were they able to induce such a state of fear within him?

Given his stature and the type of work he did, Paul was not a man accustomed to being intimidated.

"I've had gang members and hardened criminals get in my face and try to bully me. I've been threatened with guns, knives and every kind of nasty act you can think of, and it never phased me. Then a pair of weird kids show up and they have me shaking. I just don't understand it."

Unfortunately, I didn't have a solid answer for Paul as to exactly what the black eyed children were. There was little information available about the kids at the time. A few popular stories had circulated online, but they offered few specific details. Opinions were split between those who believed it was all a hoax, and those who felt the children were demons or aliens.

One of the people Paul confided in was a priest. *"Even he didn't really have any answers for me. He seemed to think they were something demonic, but I don't know, maybe he was just hoping to convert me,"* Paul joked. *"While they did feel very sinister to me, I just can't bring myself to believe in demons."*

"It's not easy for someone like me," he said. *"I've always been a skeptic about things like this. I'm the guy who would kind of snort and laugh when I heard someone talking about a UFO sighting or thinking their house was haunted. This though, this thing that happened to me, those kids, they've changed my perspective on things because I know what I saw, what I experienced, and there's no rational explanation for it."*

Paul was the first person I personally spoke with who

encountered the children. Secondhand stories were questionable, but here was a direct witness to these dark-eyed beings, and his story was compelling for many reasons. Paul was not seeking publicity or attention; he was searching for personal answers to help him come to terms with his experience. While he did agree to let me use his story, he did not want any personal information divulged that would lead to him.

Paul's attitude turned out to be a common one among those who encountered the BEKs. Witnesses seem to be reluctant to speak about their encounters for fear of ridicule or damage to their professional standing.

In the years following his encounter, Paul did some research trying to find some answers. Left in the uncomfortable position of having no explanation for his experience, he did make a few changes in his life. While he refused to believe in demons, he nevertheless returned to the church he attended as a child.

"Guess I'm playing it safe," he said. *"If by chance these things are the work of something evil, I just want to know that I'm on the right side."*

Paul also threw himself into additional training on both the physical and psychological level.

"I learned a whole lot about fear responses and how they affect the body from the mental aspects to the physical reactions. I just don't like how I responded that day when the kids knocked on the door. I never want another situation like that to happen again. I have a wife and child and I want to know that I'm capable of handling anything that might threaten my family."

Paul told me he added security cameras to monitor the front and back doors of his house. *"If by any chance those kids come back, I want it on tape."*

I still speak to Paul on occasion. He says he's moved on as best as he can, but the children and their strange eyes still haunt him.

"Sometimes, I'll have dreams about them. I'll wake up in a sweat thinking that there was a knock at the door. Then I'll realize it was a dream and that I was remembering that night. I don't think it will ever totally leave me."

Paul's story had a personal effect on me. I'd had an interest in the paranormal since I was a child. I've constantly absorbed information about numerous topics from ghosts to UFOs to cryptozoology, but one of the strange things about the black eyed kids is that they don't fit squarely into any single category. Are they really demons? Aliens? Or are they some form of spirit manifesting in our world? I decided to explore the phenomenon and see what I could discover. Since Paul had come forward, I figured I could find other people who would share their experiences. My first stop on the journey was square one, the Internet and the various popular BEK tales.

After Bethel's account was posted online, a number of other disturbing encounters made the rounds on various Internet sites. The stories, at the least, are a vital part of the lore that has grown up around the BEKs, and they are an important component in the modern perception of the phenomenon.

Internet Tales

The Internet is filled with stories involving black eyed beings. Endless websites recount reports ranging from brief sightings to full-length stories of encounters with the BEKs. Most of the stories are posted anonymously by people wanting to share their experiences. Often they hope to gain more understanding about what they have witnessed.

The accounts below represent a portion of what is out there for the public to view. These reports can be found in full on the Internet with simple searches. For the most part, they are found on websites that focus on the paranormal. They are also some of the most common accounts and are considered the 'standards' of modern BEK lore. These accounts were posted in the aftermath of the Bethel encounter. To date, as far as I'm aware, no investigators have been able to follow up on these accounts or interview the witnesses. As such, we must take them for what they are; a part of the "urban legend" aspect of the black eyed kids.

The Marine's Tale

One of the most popular BEK accounts published online involved a Marine from North Carolina listed under the forum as user name 'Reaper 3-1.'

In his posting, Reaper 3-1 claimed to be a Marine stationed at Camp Lejeune in Jacksonville, North Carolina. Camp Lejeune is the largest Marine Corps base on the east coast of the United States. His account begins:

"I live in the infantry barracks off of river road and I recently had a rather strange encounter with a pair of black eyed kids," reported the Marine.

"I live on the third floor of the barracks that have open walkways on the outside and the rooms on the inside. This happened on a weekend back in November 2009. It was a weekend, so almost every Marine was out, either home, drinking or sleeping; only a handful were left in the barracks awake. I'd stayed in that weekend because I was broke and had no money to go out."

"I was watching a movie when I heard a knock at my door. Figuring it was my roommate who'd lost his key again, I went and opened it. Instead of a drunken roommate, I found two little kids standing on the walkway— only these kids freaked the hell out of me. I don't know what it was about them, but as a Marine, we're always told to listen to that little voice in your head because it just might save your life from an IED (improvised explosive device). Right then, that voice was screaming at me to shut the door and lock it. There was also the fact that these kids had absolutely pitch-black eyes. I mean no white or any other color to them whatsoever—just black."

One of the interesting aspects of Reaper 3-1's story is that he refers to the 'little voice' in his head warning him that something was wrong with the situation. Like many people, he fought against the response because he was only being confronted with children, or at least, that's what they appeared to be. He continued:

"I pushed those things aside and asked them what they were doing there so late. They responded by saying that it was really cold out and they wanted to come in and read. I was confused as hell, because I've never met a kid that wants to read. Also, there was no mention of any parents or anything else you'd expect a lost couple of kids to say."

Clearly, the Marine was confronted with the same dilemma faced by many people who encounter the BEKs. Children, who should be innocent, putting off a menacing energy. He became fixated on the kid's black eyes and couldn't stop looking at them. There were no adults in sight and the children's requests were unusual.

"It was like they were sucking me in," he said. *"I felt horrible and was suddenly frightened for my life, like I needed to immediately take cover."*

Clearly, the young Marine was deeply disturbed by the children. *"They just kept staring at me,"* he recalled.

He looked up and down the walkway outside his room to see if any other Marines were in sight. Seeing no one else, he turned back to the kids who had apparently taken a step forward.

"I got the feeling like I was being hunted, like these kids were predators and out for their next meal or something. Instinct gave way to reason and I decided to listen to that voice and shut the door and locked it."

For the next five minutes or so, he heard a constant knocking on his door. There was a brief pause. Then he heard his window rattle as though the kids were trying to get in. After a few moments of this, things went quiet.

The Marine, of course, attempted to follow up on his experience. The next day he talked to the duty officer to find out if the man had seen any kids around. The officer dismissed the question saying he had seen nothing, no doubt thinking the Marine had simply had too much to drink and was imagining things.

If the account is true, then Reaper 3-1's story is stunning when you consider the training and mindset of the average Marine. These are not men who scare easily. In fact, as part of one of the finest fighting forces in the world, this man's story becomes even more interesting. Despite attempts, I have been unable to locate 'Reaper 3-1' so I can't verify any details of his account. I have, however, spoken to a number of other servicemen and women who have encountered the black eyed kids, and there are similar elements to their stories.

Tee's Account

According to her postings, 'Tee' is a forty-seven-year-old apartment manager who encountered a black eyed boy in Portland, Oregon. She had worked at her job for twenty years and had met a wide variety of people. She had never encountered anything like the black eyed boy though. Tee recounted her meeting with him:

"He was a young boy of about seventeen or eighteen, approximately. He asked me about an open apartment for rent. I remember feeling very scared and shaken by his appearance. He did not look weird by his dress or such. It was his eyes. I remember feeling the hair on my neck stand up, and I was

shaking just from looking in his eyes."

Tee felt a sense of dread come over her when confronted by the black eyed being, and she found it difficult to even look at him directly:

"I could not look him straight in the eyes. I felt like I was about to die. Now, some people may think that I was just over-reacting or something, but the eyes were completely black, like there was no real pupil. He spoke normally to me, but I had to just shut the door in his face and get as far from him as I could. I felt like I was in extreme danger."

Oddly, Tee recalled that she shook for hours after dealing with the young man. Her encounter also took place during the day, which is unusual for BEK encounters. She reported that she is still haunted by the image of the boy's black eyes.

Chris's Story

While less common in general, there are some accounts from people who have run into black eyed adults. Such is the case with 'Chris' who was traveling with her husband in Michigan. The couple made a stop at a rest area on I-75. What she thought was a normal trip took a turn towards the strange. When she came out of the ladies' restroom, Chris found herself face-to-face with a thin, dark-haired woman. The woman was standing outside of the bathroom staring at Chris. Chris was stunned to observe that the woman's eyes were solid black. Seeing the woman staring at her was unnerving:

"The eyes were completely black. I instantly felt a terrible sense of dread as though there was something deeply unnatural about her," recounted Chris.

She was compelled to get away from the woman as quickly as she could. She recalled the woman's stare as *"devoid of any emotion other than something very cold and disconnected."*

Like the accounts of black eyed kids, the woman exuded sinister energy. Although the woman didn't say anything, Chris became very disturbed by her appearance and the way in which the woman stood still, staring at her. The witness in this case also reported feeling an overwhelming sense of dread when confronted with the black eyed woman.

"My instant and unwavering feeling during this whole experience was that she was not human. There was something almost predatory about her as though she was homing in on prey while she stood there so still. I also had a strange sense of her feeling superior or stronger in some way. It seemed important, for some unknown reason, for me to act unaffected by her while in her presence. I felt a huge sense of relief as soon as I got back into the car and we left."

Coffee Shop Encounter

Finally, there's an account of a black eyed being in a Starbuck's coffee shop. As a national chain that fuels thousands of dedicated coffee drinkers everywhere, the coffee shop is a hub of daily activity from open to close.

The story involves a young woman who purchased a cup of tea and was on the way out to her car. The young woman stopped for a moment to retrieve her keys which had fallen to the bottom of her purse. She set the bag down on an open table and started going through it when the strange experience occurred.

"I felt like I was being watched," she said, *"so, I turned around to give whatever to the perv that I assumed was watching me."*

Any thoughts of a wise-crack died quickly however, when she was confronted with the man who was looking at her.

"I caught sight of him and made eye contact. The eyes, blacker than black, no white at all, wall-to-wall black, and I just felt a darkness around him, and evil."

The young woman saw nothing unusual about the man's attire. She described his skin tone as 'olive but pale.' His eyes and the 'aura' coming off him were what truly upset her.

"As I looked in his eyes, I somehow knew that was not a human soul occupying that body, and I felt that he knew that I knew he was not human."

The woman's report, while bearing many of the hallmarks of standard black eyed being encounters, contains several different elements. The encounter occurred during the day in a very public place. The woman stated the black eyed man was sitting at a table, and all the other tables around him were empty. As she recalled, patrons would come into the shop, see the man and purposely avoid him. He seemed to take pleasure in patrons giving him a wide berth.

While the story could be the result of someone wearing black contact lenses, it is interesting nonetheless. It gives us a certain insight into the reaction people have when faced with someone with such an odd, unsettling appearance.

There are countless other accounts to be found online with simple Internet searches. As for the earlier stories, some are detailed but most are short and simple. As awareness of the phenomenon has grown, the number of stories have increased, and so has the dramatic flair often used in sensational headlines.

But the stories beyond the Internet legends are even more fascinating. It's clear something strange is afoot. People are encountering the black eyed children around the world, from coffee shops to gas stations, from department stores to hotels. Whatever these creatures are, they are disrupting lives on a regular basis and they could knock on any door at any time.

What then, could explain their existence?

Chapter 3

Doctors & Delusional Skeptics

Medical Factors and Body Modification

I realized in short order one of my first stops for information had to be the medical profession. As stated earlier, it's important to understand if a human had solid black eyes, they would essentially be blind. But are there any conditions that could explain the *appearance* of solid, black eyes? In short, the answer is no. While there are several conditions that can alter the eyes and coloring of the eyes, such conditions don't explain what people are describing in BEK encounters.

After speaking with medical professionals, and as a matter of due diligence, I include here a brief synopsis of the main medical conditions that can affect the appearance of the eyes. Each of these conditions is considered rare and a number of factors would have to be present for any one of these medical conditions to even come close to explaining a black eyed child. It's also important to note the conditions DO NOT eliminate the whites of the eyes. So we would have to assume that all the BEK witnesses have been mistaken and that they merely missed seeing the whites of the eyes in the children they encountered.

Mydriasis

Mydriasis is an excessive dilation of the pupil. The condition can be caused by disease or trauma. Occasionally the use of certain drugs can create the condition but this is usually based on an individual's reaction to the drug.

Under normal conditions, the pupil dilates in the dark and constricts in the light. This protects the retina during daylight hours and improves visibility at night. A pupil that is mydriatic will stay in an 'open' state remaining large even under bright conditions. The appearance resulting from this condition is sometimes referred to as a 'blown pupil.'

People suffering from mydriasis often develop a high intolerance to bright light. Special sunglasses, or occasionally contact lenses are prescribed to help with the condition.

Some drugs used in eye examinations can temporarily cause a mydriatic effect. It should be noted, however, that mydriasis is not very common, nor does it cause the whites of the eyes to vanish. Additionally, the mydriatic pupil usually retains the original color of the eye. There have been no reported cases of mydriasis turning someone's eye completely black.

Glaucoma Treatment

New medicine developed in recent years to treat glaucoma has been found to have an effect on eye color. Doctors consider this a very strange side effect and it has only been found in around fifteen percent of patients taking the medication. In these cases, blue, green and hazel eyes have all turned brown after a year of using the medication. Those who have experienced such a color change, and discontinued the medication, find that the eye does not revert to its original color, so at this time, it seems the color change is permanent.

Again, this effect is on the pupil of the eye and there are no documented cases stating that the eyes have turned black.

Aniridia

The Greek term "Aniridia" translates to 'without an iris.' The condition therefore, is the absence of the iris.

Aniridia is a rare condition, usually congenital, that typically affects both eyes. Those suffering from aniridia find their vision severely limited. The disease is associated with several ocular complications. Aniridia is a hereditary disease and has been associated with Gillespie Syndrome. Many patients have been found to suffer from mental retardation and WAGR (Wilms tumour, Aniridia, Genitourinary anomalies and Range of abilities) Syndrome. In some individuals, aniridia is associated with cancer of the kidneys.

Treatments for the condition of aniridia include the prescription of a black contact lens that covers the entire cornea. Aniridia is considered an extremely rare disease and those suffering from it are usually undergoing treatment for other conditions associated with the condition.

Recreational Drug Use

There is a common argument that the use of so called 'recreational drugs' may be the cause of the black eyed kid phenomenon. While the use of drugs does indeed affect the eyes of the user, it does not explain the appearance of the BEKs. Drugs like cocaine can cause the pupils to dilate and the eyes can become watery and wide in appearance. Marijuana, on the other hand, often gives the eyes a 'sleepy' appearance. The user may have difficulty keeping the eyes fully open and there may be sensitivity to bright lights. Although drug use usually causes the eyes to take on a bloodshot appearance, there are no drugs reputed to turn the eye, including the sclera, black.

It should also be noted that drug use is usually accompanied by numerous other side effects. Nervousness, paranoia, extreme reactions - ranging from anger to laughter and slurred speech - are just a few of the signs exhibited by drug users. Someone under the influence of drugs would find it nearly impossible to maintain the calm, composed approach that black eyed children seem to exhibit to witnesses.

It's highly unlikely that medical patients are roaming the streets attempting to enter random homes while undergoing treatment for any of the above conditions. Likewise, drug users are not apt to be terrorizing strangers simply for a thrill. Most of them are busy looking for their next fix, or too paranoid of being caught to attempt such actions. When a person under the influence of drugs does approach a home for illicit reasons, they don't ask for permission to enter and such stories usually find their way onto the nightly news.

It should also be noted that head trauma, and excessive internal bleeding in the head area, can cause blood to pool in the eyes. There is in fact, a famous "real" photograph of a black eyed child that made the rounds on the Internet. The true story behind the image is a tragic one, as it was a picture captured of a child who had suffered head trauma during a natural disaster. A violent blow to the head sent blood rushing through the victim's brain, causing the eyes to turn solid black. The unfortunate child did not survive very long.

The medical conditions listed above are not ones that would allow a person to walk about freely as they all require some degree of treatment to prevent the conditions from becoming worse.

Altering the Eyes

Coloring the Cornea

Although few people are aware of it, tattooing of the cornea has been practiced for 2000 years. The practice was first described in 450 A.D., and first mentioned by Roman physician Galen of Pergamun. At that time, the practice was considered cosmetic. The physician would cauterize the corneal surface with heat. After cauterization, dye would be applied to the eye. A variety of dyes were used including iron, pulverized pomegranate bark and copper salt. The dyes would stain the corneas, effecting a cosmetic change in the appearance of the patient.

In 1869, Oculoplastic surgeon Louis Von Wecker began using black India ink to achieve the same effect. Cocaine was used to numb the eye, then a heavy solution of ink was applied to the cornea.

In the modern day, several methods are in use. In general, a dyeing agent is applied directly to the cornea. The physician inserts a needle into the eye to inject the dye directly into the cornea.

This is a very dangerous medical procedure and is only performed on rare occasions to improve vision. Patients suffering from conditions such as circumstantial glare within the iris can benefit from the procedure. This surgery is rarely used, as there are many risks associated with it, including complete blindness. It's a difficult procedure and must be performed precisely by a highly trained professional. Usually, patients who opt for the procedure are already nearly blind. Toxic reactions are common and the tattooed area may fade or reduce in size after time.

Tattooing of the Sclera

Another practice similar to corneal tattooing is the tattooing of the sclera, or 'white of the eye.' While corneal tattooing is done for medical reasons, tattooing of the sclera is considered a body modification process.

In 2007, extreme practitioner of body modification, Pauly Unstoppable, became the first recorded person to have the whites of his eyes tattooed as part of his ongoing body modification. Soon after, two prisoners undertook the procedure to have the whites of their eyes colored red and blue.

This extreme body modification practice is fairly new and is considered very dangerous. Only a physician or skillful tattoo master can perform the procedure. Even so, there are numerous risks including infection, perforation of the eye, hemorrhage and complete or partial blindness.

Tattoo artists willing to perform the process claim it's relatively painless since the surface of the eye does not contain any nerve endings. However, there are aftereffects from undergoing this dangerous process. Bruising, pain in the eye, general discomfort and the feeling of something stuck in the eye are all potential side effects.

In the modern process, dye is inserted directly into the sclera. A needle is covered with ink and the eye is punctured with the needle. The ink is then injected directly into the sclera, dyeing the white part of the eye.

Citing the dangers of this experimental practice, the state of Oklahoma passed a bill banning the practice of eyeball tattooing in 2009. Tattooing of the eye is a very limited practice and there are no reports of children or teenagers having received the procedure for body modification.

Debunking the Skeptics

I have no issue with logical thought and careful investigation. In fact it's vital when approaching the paranormal field. Great care must be taken in conducting interviews, research and fieldwork, and every measure should be taken to ensure accuracy. True skeptics are a boon to research and an asset to science, it's the armchair fringe skeptic who will call a red sign blue just for spite, sensationalism and attention. These fringe armchair skeptics are some of the most fervent 'believers' I've ever met. Indeed, they are so desperate to force you to 'see the light,' that they rival Jehovah's Witnesses in their endless pursuit of promoting their word. (Nothing against Jehovah's Witnesses mind you; their persistence can be admirable.)

For the most part, I find these brand of skeptics aren't genuinely interested in interviewing witnesses or investigating cases beyond their armchairs and keyboards. They approach any kind of unexplained phenomena with the preconceived belief that it's either a hoax, or pure ignorance on the part of the witnesses. In fact, their main activity seems to be issuing proclamations and woe to anyone who doesn't simply take them at their word.

Of course, skeptics love the BEKs. The "explanation" most promoted by the scientifically enlightened skeptical crowd to solve the black eyed kid mystery is that they are physical children out playing a prank on adults. They accomplish this by purchasing solid black contact lenses and wearing them while knocking on the doors of strangers. Paul, whose encounter I discussed earlier, spent time exploring the possibility of black contacts.

"I found a set of those things through a costume supply company," he said.

"I had to special order them and it took a while to get them in. I'll admit, when I first opened them up and saw them, I thought, maybe this was a possible explanation. Then I tried them on. The things had my eyes raw and itchy after only a few minutes, they just weren't well made. Now, let me point out that I've worn prescription contacts before myself so it wasn't a matter of not being used to wearing something like this. Unlike regular contacts though, they seemed thicker, maybe because of the color. My eyes got very red

around the edges and I just couldn't get them to sit comfortably in the eye. Maybe that's because they're generic, not tailored to my eye at all. Not only was there an issue with discomfort, I found that they actually severely limited my eye movement and made it hard to use my peripheral vision."

Going a few steps further, Paul put the contacts on one evening right around the time he encountered the kids at his home.

"Well, I made sure no one was around first. Then I stood outside, just like those kids did that evening. With the light fading, it made it even harder to see well. It was worse than wearing sunglasses in the dark because at least then you've got good peripheral vision—not with these things, though. Not only that, but trying to get off the porch quickly was damn near impossible."

Paul's comments raised some interesting points and I decided to gather some other opinions on the possible use of black contacts. There are a lot of companies that sell specialty contact lenses via the Internet. They sell more than just black ones, and I'm told that currently, the most popular designs are the 'zombie' lenses with various colored designs.

While some people seem to have no issue wearing the lenses, there are also a fair number of complaints, the most common being that the contacts cause tunnel vision. This is the same loss of peripheral vision Paul experienced when he tried the lenses out.

Attending a horror/paranormal convention, I had an opportunity to speak with many people who had purchased colored lenses at the show. Just over half the people I asked reported problems wearing the lenses.

"They really aren't comfortable," reported Shelly, a young lady wearing red sclera lenses. *"I keep bumping into things. They don't fit my eyes very well and I won't be able to keep them in long."*

Dealers at the show told me it's rare to sell the lenses to kids, part of the reason being the price point. The sclera lenses aren't cheap and the people who are buying them usually do so to complete a more elaborate costume.

(I should note here, when I first researched this topic, the lenses were much more expensive. In recent years, the popularity of costumes and "cosplay" have driven prices down and black contacts can now be had for around 30-50 dollars a pair, a far cry from prices just a few years ago).

Dialogue with a Skeptic

My most amusing exchange with a skeptical view of the BEKs came from a self-professed 'expert' in the paranormal field, a skeptic, who had a 'rational' explanation for every aspect of the encounters.

I spoke with Ted numerous times in person and via telephone and Internet. Frankly, the conversations became more absurd the further they progressed. He's a good representative of the armchair, fringe skeptical approach and their explanation for black eyed child encounters.

Ted contacted me early in my research into BEK sightings. He continued to contact me over time, almost desperate to convince me to view the sightings the same way he did, as nothing but a large-scale hoax. The exchange below is culled from several conversations with Ted over the course of my research.

"The black eyed children are simply a bunch of teenagers having a good time," Ted told me. He assured me, in no uncertain terms, there was nothing strange or paranormal about the BEKs.

"The so called black eyed kids are all teenagers who are doing it for a thrill. They purchase black contacts and usually wear what they call 'Goth' clothes." (Apparently, Ted considered hoodies "goth" attire.) *"They go to stranger's houses, knock on the door and show those black eyes to the person who answers. Then they just run off when the person isn't looking."*

Ted didn't sound very familiar with the average BEK report. I found no accounts of black eyed children dressed in typical Goth clothing, the one subculture I would expect to be attracted to such things.

Ted was so convinced by his own 'expertise' on the topic, I decided to see just how far he could push his explanation and remain rational.

"So, Ted," I asked, *"How and where are these kids getting the black contacts?"*

"Oh, that's easy" he replied. *"They order them online; costume supply stores have them."*

I knew this of course since I had researched the possibility.

"Okay, but isn't that a little pricey for a one-off gag?" I asked. (A

quick check at that time, on current prices for black sclera contacts—a contact that covers the white of the eye—revealed an average price point of about one hundred and thirty dollars per lens).

"Nah, they use their parents' credit cards anyway."

So, around $260.00 for a pair of black contact lenses to hopefully scare someone for a couple of minutes. The argument was on thin ice already. Would most parents not notice this chunk of change on their credit cards? I asked Ted where he thought the idea had come from to begin with.

"Oh, it was a fad that some teenager started and posted on the Internet. So, it got them all doing it."

My big question of course was about motivation.

"So, Ted, what's the purpose behind all of this? Why would these kids spend time and money on such antics when no one knows they're doing it? Where's the satisfaction in that kind of stunt and why is it happening all over the country and now, abroad?"

"Look, they're getting plenty of thrills out of it," he replied.. *"These kids are all part of Internet discussion groups. They go online and post their stories about who they've scared, how they did it and how the people reacted."*

Now, finally, Ted had said something that sounded interesting. I thought, for a brief moment, that if this were indeed the case, then it could explain at least a portion of the black eyed kid encounters. Not only that, it would be easy enough to verify.

"I'd love to see some of those postings Ted; can you send me the links?"

"Oh, well," there was a pause, *"I don't have links to any of those sites."*

"Well, you said that's where the kids are posting their stories," I replied. *"I assumed you had read some of the accounts."*

"Yes, well, a fellow skeptic informed me about the postings. I don't have any of the links myself."

Now I was really amused. This was the very thing skeptics claimed other people did, passing along secondhand information, using 'facts' that weren't really facts. I'd done extensive research on the Internet and I had never found anything remotely similar to the groups Ted was referring to.

The deeper into the conversation we went, the more absurd the explanations became. It turns out Ted believed in a vast conspiracy of teenagers and pre-teens who were taking their parents' credit cards to purchase $260 dollars worth of black contacts. Donning the black lenses, they would travel to strange neighborhoods so they weren't recognized and knock on random doors. Once they had frightened the occupants, they would use expert timing to dash around the corner of the house when the person wasn't looking, effectively 'disappearing.'

Their satisfaction came through rushing home and posting details of the escapade on an Internet discussion site, set up specifically for the black eyed kid hoaxers. Apparently, the sites are super-secret and hidden from Internet searches. This is a growing hobby that adults have not discovered and which now stretches not only from coast-to-coast but also overseas.

I sometimes wonder if skeptics realize they bend more of the laws of nature in attempting to debunk something than those who may believe in the paranormal do to support their beliefs. Ted's rambling explanation for the BEKs is a perfect example of this kind of behavior.

Having raised kids myself, I know it's challenging to get them to take the trash out on time, let alone participate in some vast conspiracy on a global scale. Not only that, average teenagers spend most of their time on cell phones, tablets and other electronic devices. The attention span of most of today's youth simply isn't focused on long-term pranks and grand conspiracies.

For the sake of following up all leads, I did speak with several teenagers to try to get some answers. I also employed a pair of teens with an interest in the paranormal to follow up on their own among their peers. Not a single teen knew of, or expressed any interest in, spending the time and money needed for such an elaborate hoax. Ted's argument proved to be pure nonsense.

Modern teenagers derive much more satisfaction from video games, going out with their friends and learning about the complexities of young romance.

With no forums or chat rooms to be found on the Internet, and no teenagers interested in time-consuming pranks, I shared my information with Ted the skeptic the next time he rang. I requested again that he direct me to the mythical Internet groups, pressing him to retrieve the information from his friend. He listened quietly and when he finally spoke, I could hear the frustration in his voice.

"Listen to me; you're wasting your time with all this nonsense. There's no such thing as black eyed children. Everyone who tells one of these stories is either the victim of a hoax, they were mistaken, or they're lying."

Ah, the skeptic's greatest weapon, when all else fails, issue a proclamation!

Obviously, if you've experienced something you can't explain, it's either a trick being played on you, you're stupid, or you've fabricated the entire incident. It's almost surprising that the swamp gas argument hasn't been brought out to explain the BEKs.

I find such contempt toward people very distasteful. I have no doubt there are hoaxers out there, seeking attention, and hoping to see their names printed somewhere.

However, the majority of people I have interviewed about the black eyed children aren't looking for attention. They don't want to see their names in the papers and they don't want to be on television talking about their encounter. They just want to understand. The skeptic's way of helping people is to try to convince them they were duped, mistaken, plain stupid, or are out-and-out liars.

After conducting countless interviews with people who have had direct experience with these weird children, I'm convinced there's some reality behind the BEKs. The witnesses are experiencing something that is currently unexplained. But, are there hoaxes involving people with black eyes? Most certainly. Probably a few adults here and there who were trying to get a rise out of friends and relatives.

Are the black eyed kids merely an urban legend? No. There are simply too many direct encounters with the kids for them to fit the mold of urban myth and numerous, credible first-hand accounts.

.

Chapter 4

Through The Black Eyes Of History

Historical accounts of black eyed children are difficult to find. In part, this is because the terms 'black eyed children' and 'BEKs' are recent. It's the advent of the Internet and the growing number of accounts that have led to these specific terms for the strange children. In the past, black eyes were only a part of the overall story, not the prominent feature. A being with black eyes may have been interpreted as a ghost, demon, vampire or other supernatural entity depending on specific details and location of the story. In older accounts, cultural beliefs played an important part in how the beings were classified.

Asia's Vengeful Ghosts

Traveling in China years ago, I occasionally heard tales that included beings with black eyes. At times, these tales involved spirits known in China as 'hungry ghost.' Other times, the tales were related to mythical creatures from the region's folklore.

At the time, I looked at the tales in the context in which they were told, a fascinating part of the region's lore. Ghost stories were common, and if the spirit was malevolent, it would often have red or black eyes. The eyes were never presented as the focus of the tale. It was merely additional evidence from the storyteller to affirm the spirit was evil.

41

We must wonder how such classical stories fit in with modern accounts of the BEKs. Have the black eyed beings been here much longer than most people currently believe?

I recall being told a story in southern China. It was the tale of an angry spirit terrorizing a nearby village and bringing misfortune to the people who lived there. The ghost was of a young girl angry at her wrongful death. No one seemed to know who the girl was, how or when she had died, or who was to blame. The people held the ghost of the girl responsible for numerous disasters and misfortunes in the area. To see the spirit of the girl meant one was about to experience bad fortune. Miscarriages and infant deaths were said to be a result of close encounters with the dreadful spirit. If there were no babies in the family, the person encountering the spirit girl would lose their youngest relative.

The ghost was described as a young girl around fourteen to sixteen years of age. She would appear in the village late at night. Often, she would knock on doors, asking to be let in. She could appear suddenly, and most people believed it wasn't safe to stay out too late, especially if the moon was full. The angry spirit always wore a long white dress and was barefoot. She had long black hair and her skin was deathly pale. Her eyes were solid black.

The villagers believed they would be haunted by the girl until the mystery of her death was solved, and the nature of her wrongful passing was corrected. Fortune tellers tried to determine the nature of the curse to no avail. Finally, a Taoist priest was called to the village to exorcise the evil spirit. He determined the nature of the girl's death and why she continued to linger. He cleansed the area and forced the vengeful spirit to move on, setting her soul at ease.

By all accounts, the ritual was successful. The town's fortunes changed dramatically after the exorcism, and after the ceremony, sightings of the girl's spirit ceased. The town believed the vengeful ghost had finally been put to rest.

This Chinese tale bears many similarities to Onryo (vengeful ghost) stories from Japan. Onryo tales date back to the eighth century and are based on the concept that angry spirits of the dead influence the world of the living. Onryo tales usually involve the murder of a woman whose spirit becomes an Onryo and returns to the physical world in order to seek vengeance. In these popular ghost stories, the vengeful spirit is usually described as a woman attired in a white dress with pale, white skin. Her eyes are usually distorted in some way, often one eye is much larger than the other. In some modern versions Onryo are depicted with solid black eyes.

Tales of black-eyed beings can in fact be found in the folklore of numerous Asian cultures. Most often, they are used to represent angry ghosts or spirits seeking revenge.

Japanese movie makers have made use of the creepy effect of solid black eyes in recent horror movies. In truth, they are drawing from the rich cultural lore of Japan and its many tales of ghosts, demons and spirits. While often classified as mere folklore, Japanese tales of various beings are woven all throughout the country's cultural landscape and have long been an important part of the culture.

Clearly, the natural assumption that black eyes are associated with something unnatural and likely evil crosses cultural barriers and beliefs and spans the ages.

Harold's Story

Crossing the globe back to America, there's an early account I uncovered that falls within the parameters of typical BEK encounters. From a rural area of Virginia along the eastern shore, the tale is one of the most interesting accounts that have surfaced to date.

I was led to the story by a family friend. Talking late one night about my research into modern black eyed children accounts, my friend said his family had a story that sounded similar to the tales I was relating. His account was not a recent one, however, as it dated back to around 1950.

I was able to speak with him further along with several of his family members. Their story was one that had been passed down through the years. Each member of the family recalled the same details of the encounter.

The family, and many of its members, have lived in rural Virginia for generations as farmers and fishermen, hardworking country people, what most would call 'salt of the earth.' A now deceased relative named Harold grew up in the area in the 1950's. He lived in the region most of his life and always called the area home.

When he was sixteen years old, Harold encountered a strange

child. No one could ever explain where the boy had come from, nor was the weird boy ever reported in the area again after Harold's run-in with him.

Harold was walking home early one evening just before sundown. He was taking his time strolling along the dirt road when he reached the fence line that led to his family's home. There, leaning against the corner fence post, was a young boy of about ten to twelve years of age.

Harold slowed down, puzzled since he knew everyone in the small community, yet he had never seen this boy before. Harold had a good-natured manner and would talk to anyone about anything. When he reached the boy, he simply started talking to him. The boy didn't respond. He just stood there leaning against the post, looking slightly down toward the ground.

Receiving no response, Harold wondered if something was wrong with the boy. He stopped talking for a moment before leaning closer.

"Hey, you all right?" Harold asked.

With this, the boy finally spoke. His reply was rather blunt.

"I wanna go to your house. Take me to your house."

Harold felt a strange chill come over him at the boy's response. He wasn't sure what to say. He couldn't understand why a boy he didn't know was asking to go to his house.

At that moment, the young boy looked up directly at Harold. It was then he realized the young boy's eyes were solid black. There was not a speck of white showing in the eyes.

Harold began to feel very afraid. He looked up the drive toward his house. He felt rooted to the spot for some reason, but his thoughts were focused on how fast he could run to his home. Harold's thoughts seemingly produced a further comment from the strange black eyed boy. The child scowled at him and said coldly:

"Now, don't you run away from me. You're gonna walk me to your house."

The comment seemed like a threat, and it was the final straw for Harold. He launched into a mad dash up the drive toward his house.

He was running as hard as he could and didn't look back for fear the weird child was following him.

Part way up the drive, Harold heard a strange call behind him. It sounded like the scream of a bobcat. Of course, the screeching sound only served to help Harold's legs move faster in the rush to reach his home. *"I think I must have really angered that boy,"* Harold later commented. *"He screamed out and I thought for sure he was coming to get me."*

Once safely in the house, Harold slammed the door behind him. His parents, seeing him so out of breath, asked what was wrong. He told them about his encounter with the creepy boy. Thinking he would get to the bottom of things, Harold's father promptly walked down the driveway with a shotgun in hand, but found no sign of the boy his son had described.

Harold's parents listened to their son recount the story a second time, asking a few questions along the way. Since their son was never one to make up stories, his parents believed the tale. Harold insisted the child he encountered was solid and could not have been a ghost.

His father simply wasn't sure what to make of the encounter. While he had heard strange tales in the country, he'd never heard of anything like the black eyed kid his son described. For her part, Harold's mother firmly believed her son had met the devil himself. To that end, she promptly had him dress in good clothes and took him to the local clergy for a blessing.

Harold's father later spoke to nearby neighbors to see if they had encountered anything strange. While a couple of area residents reported they had recently heard a bobcat, none of them had seen any out of place children. The family decided to keep the story quiet. If by chance their son had encountered the devil, they didn't want any talk about it getting around, or for that matter, anything that might cause the black eyed boy to return.

This intriguing, older tale, certainly fits the profile of many modern encounters with the black eyed children. The solid black eyes and the insistent request to be taken inside echo today's accounts of BEKs. Also, eerily familiar, is the feeling of a veiled threat being issued to the witness. Harold himself had never felt anything so sinister, though reportedly, he never did admit that he personally believed the boy was the devil.

Other aspects of the case are different from modern accounts. Harold's description of a sound, apparently emitted by the BEK, and resembling the scream of a bobcat, is somewhat unique. He believed the scream was an expression of the boy's anger at being left behind. If the sound truly came from the black eyed child, perhaps it was an expression of rage on the boy's part. While the bobcat is a small animal, their vocalization is rather loud. They emit a high-pitched scream that can be quite startling, especially to someone already in a state of panic.

Another curious and unsettling aspect of this encounter is the black eyed child's apparent ability to read Harold's mind. Perhaps this was simply a matter of reading young Harold's body language and anticipating his natural response. Disturbing encounters such as these can warp one's perceptions, so Harold may have already started moving when the comment was made, his memory altered by the stress of the event.

If we look at the account in comparison to modern attempts by the black eyed children to 'influence' people however, it takes on a different possibility. Was this child attempting to control Harold by reading his thoughts and trying to counter them? Harold stated he felt "rooted" to the spot, even though he wanted to run. This is similar to accounts wherein the victim wants to get away, but feels unable to complete the action, a type of 'brain freeze' as one witness described it:

"You know what you want, or need to do, and you're telling your body to do it, but the signal's getting lost somewhere."

The effect may be the result of hypnosis or some other form of mind control. Interesting enough, in Harold's story, as with modern accounts, the attempted influence didn't prove successful. At some point, the request became too much and fear overrode the influence that was being attempted. In Harold's case, the combination of the boy's black eyes, and the veiled threat and demands, were enough to shake him out of his temporary trance and force him to action—and flight.

Harold later told his family he wanted to forget the boy, but he was never able to get the image out of his mind. *"Those eyes, they haunted me,"* he told his children in later years. *"Nobody should have to see something like that; it scares a couple of years out of you."*

All in all, Harold's encounter is an intriguing one. It will be useful for comparison as other accounts of the black eyed kids come to light. It's very likely there are additional stories such as Harold's out there waiting to be uncovered. Hopefully, further study of the black eyed children phenomena will reveal more associated stories and give us further historical context in which to place these intriguing tales.

.

Chapter 5

Disturbing Encounters

When investigating strange phenomena, it's important to look for patterns in reported cases. Locations and times are factors, but so are connecting links among witnesses. Looking for connections in background, religious belief, even age, can lead to interesting revelations.

Over the years that I've collected accounts of the black eyed children, there have been very few connecting links among the victims of the incidents. One curious factor did arise however. There are an unusual number of encounters reported by people employed in some type of authority or service-oriented role. Nurses, firefighters, law enforcement officers, government employees, and members of the military account for a good percentage of BEK encounters.

It's difficult to determine a reason for this fact, but there are a few things to consider. Many of these jobs require long hours and are typically high stress. This being the case, there may be a correlation between working conditions and paranormal encounters. Perhaps as more black eyed kid accounts are documented, the percentage will decrease.

One would expect, due to the nature of their jobs, that these people would have a greater level of composure when faced with the strange children. For the most part, however, they react as everyone else does to varying degrees. They battle the fight or flight response, they experience fear and disbelief, and they are left haunted by the image of the children and the odd requests they issue.

I consider the following two accounts of encounters with the BEK the most impressive ones I have received to date. They are from people with a high level of training in observation, awareness and tactics.

The first is from an enlisted man whom I interviewed in person. I found John to be a smart, well-mannered man, with a strict no-nonsense attitude. Having served in the military for many years, he held the bearing of a strong-minded person with considerable respect for his country and his role in the service.

John was reluctant to talk openly about his encounter at first, having no need or association with anything paranormal. But he couldn't deny what he had experienced, nor could he discount the aftermath of the incident. He still feels haunted by the image of the strange boy he confronted, and he hopes to someday have a logical explanation for his encounter.

John's Encounter

In the spring of 2011, I was contacted by a man named John about an encounter he had with a black eyed child while traveling on the back roads of Texas.

John has been in the military for over seven years, enlisting right after high school. He considered himself a levelheaded, rational person, and never had any interest in the paranormal. His encounter occurred during a drive on a lonely Texas back road in the summer of 2009.

John's family goes back several generations in the Lone Star state. Because of their long history there, John has relatives all over Texas from east to west. Each time he got leave from the military, he'd head home to visit family.

In 2009, John went home on leave to visit his parents in the Houston area. After a couple days with them, he decided to take a drive to west Texas and visit cousins from his Dad's side of the family. John loved driving the back roads of Texas, especially late at night. There were few cars out, and he said, it gave him a sense of peace to drive under the starry sky. John was never a heavy sleeper and he could stay up for long hours without needing rest, a trait that served him well in the military.

He planned to make the trip in two legs, spending a day with a friend from high school halfway to his destination. He left his buddy's house that evening after dinner, intending to make it to his cousin's house by early morning the next day. His gas tank full, and a thermos of coffee at hand, John set out for the long trek.

"It was a perfect night," he said. *"There wasn't a cloud in the sky, so the stars were bright. I was taking my time; a lot of deer tend to cross the road late at night and I didn't want to hit one."*

Around three in the morning, John hit a long stretch of road in the western half of the state. Houses were few and far between in that part of the country. Although he felt wide-awake, he liked to drink coffee during his leisurely drives.

"I'd finished off half of the thermos that I'd refilled at a twenty-four-hour mart, and it was time to answer the call of nature." I hit a length of road that was long and straight and I could see there weren't any cars as far as you could see in either direction. There was plenty of space to pull over, so I slowed down and parked just off the side of the highway. I went a few paces away from the road and took care of my business. After that, I just stood there for a few minutes to work out the kinks and look up at the stars. Couldn't have been more than five minutes total. My eyes were pretty adjusted to the dark, enough that I had a good view of a rabbit I scared when I was walking back to the truck."*

Deciding it was time to get back on the road, John passed in front of his truck and reached for the door handle. It was then he received a shock. Standing just past the driver's door was a young boy. John jerked back with a start when he realized a figure was standing there so close by. He described the unnerving experience:

"He didn't move a muscle. I think, if my eyes hadn't been adjusted to the dark, I probably wouldn't have seen him. I realized right away that it was just a kid and that made me calm down a bit.

I shook my head and said, 'Geez kid, you scared the hell out of me!'

This kid, he didn't miss a beat, he says to me, 'I want to get in your truck.'

I didn't say anything at first; I wasn't sure what to say, to tell you the truth."

John said he felt a cold chill when he heard the boy's statement. He paused and took a breath, looking at the boy. His mind was racing, trying to piece together where the child had come from.

He turned and glanced around in each direction, looking for any sign of a house. There were none to be seen. Even out here, most people left a night light on after dark. John scanned the road too, but there were no other vehicles visible in either direction.

The boy still hadn't moved, and again repeated his cold statement.

"'I want to get in your truck now.'

"I'll tell you, the hair on the back of my neck stood up. I was having a bad, bad feeling in the pit of my stomach. I tried to reason with my brain, thinking things like, this is only a young boy out here, there's nothing I should be worried about. Nothing was working though; I couldn't kick the weird feeling that just kept getting stronger."

John tried to smile. He decided to engage the boy so he could find out what exactly was happening out on the back road and why a young boy was alone in the middle of nowhere.

"You live around here kid?"

The boy stood completely still and responded in the same monotone voice.

"Just let me get in your truck; we can go for a ride."

"Do you need to get home kid? Whereabouts do you live?"

The boy remained planted in his position between the road and John's truck, continuing to insist on a ride.

"We can get in your truck now. It won't take too long."

John leaned forward a little, looking closely at the boy. He wanted to see as many details as he could in the low light. From his height and size, John thought the boy was around the age of ten.

"The kid was wearing a dull white shirt that looked a bit too big for him. I know what hand-me-downs are like and that's what I thought this kid was wearing. The shirt was tucked into dark trousers. The boy's hair was dark, probably dark brown and it was shaggy but not long. I couldn't really see other details too well due to the low light."

Although the moon afforded some light, it was still very dark and John strained to see more details of the boy's appearance. The nervous feeling John had was growing more intense.

The boy had still not moved from his spot, but he once again repeated his request. His voice was more insistent this time, apparently in an attempt to convince John to comply.

"Just open the door and tell me to get in. We'll have a short ride."

"I just felt like I wanted to run and leave that boy and my truck as far behind as I could. I realized I was squinting my eyes and I felt like I was trying to shake off a punch or something. It was a funny feeling. I knew right then I had to get out of there. I shook my head and tried to clear my thoughts."

John looked at his truck, then back at the young boy.

"I don't think so kid," he answered.

John took a step forward, just enough to get the driver's door open. He tried to keep looking at the boy as he quickly jumped into the driver's seat. He turned to put the key in the ignition and quickly started the truck. The truck kicked over on the first try and John turned to look out through his driver's side window.

The boy was now standing beside the driver's door, peering in at John.

"I've never felt like I did the moment when that kid was glaring in the window at me. I threw the truck into gear and floored the gas."

A couple of miles down the road, John stopped the truck and pulled off the road again.

"I looked down at my hands. I was holding the steering wheel so tight that my hands were turning white. I was breathing real fast too. I took a deep breath and worked on calming myself down. All of a sudden, I felt ridiculous. I started to question myself. What in the world was I doing running from a child. Maybe that boy needed some kind of help. Maybe he was messed up in the head or something."

Something caused John's fight or flight response to kick in and he couldn't understand what had done it.

"I had a very primal response but I couldn't figure out what had caused it."

53

John composed himself for another moment, then turned the truck around. He was determined to return to the spot, find the boy, and get some answers. If the boy was hurt or in trouble, John would get him home. He put his high beams on and drove slowly back to the area where he had encountered the boy.

"I've usually got a good sense of distance and my surroundings. It only took me one pass to find the exact spot where I had pulled off the first time. I was driving slow and I had a high-powered flashlight that I was shining out of the window. I passed that light all over looking for that boy. I drove past the spot, down about a half mile and then came back. He was nowhere to be found. I thought he had to be close by, a boy that small couldn't move very fast. After a couple of passes up and down the road, I pulled back over at the exact spot where I'd parked the first time."

John got out and stood by his truck with the door open. He used his flashlight to scan the area in all directions.

"Standing on that deserted road, my mind flashed back to that boy and I suddenly saw the image of that kid staring in the window at me. It gave me a chill all over again. I got back in the truck and drove away, but I made sure to look at the next mile marker. I wanted to know where the spot was."

John had originally planned to stop for an early morning breakfast, but instead didn't quit driving until he reached his destination. It was the early hours of the morning and his relatives had left the side door unlocked for him. Knowing he couldn't sleep after the night's events, John sat down in the living room and turned on the television.

"I just wanted to distract myself with something from the normal world, something stupid and simple. I just wanted that kid out of my mind."

By late morning, John had managed to push the encounter to the back of his mind. He tried his best to enjoy time with his family.

"I'd go about my business, talking and joking around, and then that kid would pop into my head. I'd see him standing there, staring in the window of my truck. I just couldn't shake it and I couldn't understand it."

When John made his return trip to Houston, he did so during daylight hours.

"I made sure I hit that spot in the middle of the day. I stopped again too. I wanted to see if there were any houses close by that the kid could have come from."

54

John found the area where he'd had his encounter. The nearest homes were well off the beaten path, and at least a few miles from the point of his late-night talk with the boy.

John didn't linger at the spot for very long. He had no intention of being in the area when the sun went down, nor did he even want to drive after dark. In fact, John completely stopped driving at night after his encounter, suddenly preferring the bright light of day for his travels. He still feels haunted by the image of the spooky boy peering in through the window of his truck.

"I've never really gotten that image out of my head. I get rid of it for awhile but it always seems to come back around. Maybe there's some explanation, but there was nowhere for that boy to get to, nowhere for him to hide and I don't know how he made me feel so damn scared. He didn't really do anything and it doesn't make sense."

John always believed his military training had prepared him for anything, yet he found himself unprepared for his encounter with a strange child on a quiet back road in west Texas.

Because of the conditions of John's encounter, he was unable to clearly see the boy's eyes. The boy's skin, John noted, was very light and pale, showing up well in the limited light available. The level of fear John experienced during his encounter with the boy is notable, but there are other elements in the account that are in sync with common BEK accounts, such as the boy's sudden appearance and disappearance at a random location. Strange requests bordering on demands, an undertone of threat, and a growing insistence when demands are not met are all common elements of BEK behavior.

The Deputy's Account

When one thinks of professionals highly trained in observation and attention to detail, the first thing that comes to mind are members of law enforcement. When I made contact with a sheriff's deputy from the Kansas City, Missouri area, I was impressed by his no nonsense attitude and direct response to my questions. He was short and to the point when asking me questions, but when asked for specific details, was very clear and concise.

Like John, this gentleman had spent many years in his chosen profession, and has been unable to explain his odd encounter with a pair of black eyed children. The officer was another nonbeliever in the paranormal, yet he could not explain his encounter as anything but unnatural. His experience occurred in early 2003.

As one would expect from a law enforcement officer, he was careful to note details of the children he encountered. Here's the account as he related it to me:

"I received a call on a domestic disturbance just after two AM on a Tuesday. Reaching the neighborhood, I found that the argument had quieted down for the most part. I dealt with the parties involved and no arrests were made. I returned to my car parked on the street in front of the house, finished some paperwork, and radioed in. Glancing up, I noticed that there was someone standing on the porch just a couple of doors down from my call. The porch light was on and I could tell that these were young people. I got out of my car and began to approach, realizing as I did that they were two young kids. I was concerned that youngsters were outside so late and I called out to them. They did not respond although they were looking in my direction. I continued to speak to them as I approached the house.

'You kids alright? Did the noise wake you up?'

This porch, actually more of a deck, had a railing that ran all the way around, with the steps on the right side. I climbed the steps and looked closely at the kids, one boy and one girl. I guessed their ages to be between eight and ten years, the boy appeared slightly older. The light on the deck was fairly bright so I was able to get a good look at the kids.

Their clothing looked old, possibly handmade, and they had very pale complexions. I tried to speak to them again, but they still wouldn't answer my questions. They just stood there almost in the middle of the deck, to the left of the front door. I bent down to be a bit closer and asked them again if they needed help.

There was a pause, but finally, the boy responded.

'We want to go inside.'

It sounded a little like he had an accent, but not one I could place. He looked straight at me and it was then I realized that it wasn't just the light; these kids had completely black eyes.

I've never seen anything like this. I wondered if these little kids were on some kind of drugs.

'Why did you come outside?' I asked. 'Did the noise wake you up?'

The boy responded again. 'They won't let us inside.'

I felt very disturbed by the behavior of these children. Were they mentally ill? Perhaps this was an abuse situation. The kids looked rather pale to me; perhaps they were malnourished. Something was setting off my warning signals but I wasn't sure exactly what was wrong here. I needed to get some answers from the homeowners. I opened the screen door and knocked on the front door, identifying myself as an officer with the Sheriff's department. There didn't appear to be any lights on in the house. I looked at the kids and they were just standing there, side-by-side, staring at me. They hadn't budged the whole time. I waited a moment and knocked on the door again, this time louder. The situation was strange and I was going to get to the bottom of it. I knocked a third time, calling out loudly and identifying myself again as being from the Sheriff's office and requesting the occupants to open up.

When I glanced back over at the kids, I discovered that they were gone.

The deck wasn't that big and they couldn't have moved past me because I was blocking the steps while holding the door open. They would have had to have climbed the railing and jumped into the yard. I turned my flashlight on and searched the yard. I searched the whole front yard with my light. There were no trees, and nothing that could have hidden the children. They had just vanished.

The front door opened and an elderly woman was standing there in her nightgown. She had clearly been asleep. I questioned her about the children and she assured me that she lived alone, had no small children of her own, nor did she have any grandchildren. I described the children to her but she didn't believe that the description matched any of the neighborhood kids. I searched the yard front and back, as well as the adjoining properties. Furthermore, I cruised around the surrounding blocks, but I found no sign of the children anywhere.

On several other occasions, I went to the same neighborhood hoping to spot the same kids, and find out what exactly was going on. I never saw them again but I've never let go of what I witnessed. I even checked with child protective services, figuring that kids like that were probably in the system, but no such luck.

I still go back to that neighborhood on occasion. I've cruised around it during the day and late at night. I've even went back in the early morning hours to see if those children were out again by chance. I feel like I'll never have a satisfactory answer as to where those kids came from."

Although the deputy kept his encounter quiet and never discussed it with his fellow officers, he continues to pay attention, waiting for the day when one of them may have an encounter with the black eyed kids.

PART 2:

The Theories

Chapter 6

The Hybrid Question

It's obvious to anyone looking at artistic depictions of the black eyed kids that they bear a striking resemblance to another denizen of the paranormal world, the so-called 'gray aliens.'

While the eyes are the central focus of attention, and most memorable feature on the face of both beings, there are also other similarities. Like the gray aliens, the black eyed children are often reported to have odd colored skin, sometimes with a strange texture causing it to look artificial. The BEKs are also usually reported as being very thin or lean, though at times this is hidden by baggy or ill-fitting clothing.

The various similarities between the two entities have, in part, led to speculation the BEKs are some type of alien-human hybrid.

The Gray Aliens

In 1987, author Whitley Strieber released his book *"Communion: A True Story."* The book was an account of Strieber's experiences with nonhuman beings. The possible extraterrestrial origins of the entities inspired the cover painting by artist Ted Seth Jacobs. The painting has become iconic in the UFO field and is probably the most widely recognized cultural image of the 'gray aliens.'

The startling painting is a close up of a gray, its skin is smooth and pale, its large head sits atop a thin neck, and there is no facial hair. The facial features are small except for the oversized, solid black eyes.

Gazing out at shoppers from bookshelves around the country, the strange image struck a chord and became the accepted face of the mysterious aliens that became known as the grays.

Seth based his painting on descriptions from Strieber's encounters. Details in alien encounter reports from around the world are consistent in terms of the grays. They are described as having small bodies, smooth skin, an enlarged head and solid, black eyes. The eyes are often described as shiny or glossy. The aliens do not appear to have any sex organs, and they do not exhibit any muscular definition.

Although, due to the success of Communion, there's a common belief that the image of the grays was created starting with the encounters documented by Whitley Strieber, the depiction of the aliens is extremely similar to those described by legendary science fiction writer, H. G. Wells. In his 1901 novel, *"The First Men In The Moon,"* Wells described the 'Selenites,' aliens native to the moon. In the novel, the Selenites had gray skin, big, oversized heads and large black eyes.

Modern claims of close encounters with the gray aliens often speak in detail about the eyes of the creatures. These modern grays have no noticeable outer nose or ears, and the mouth opening is described as very small. Hence, the oversized black eyes are accented more and are the singular feature that stands out in witness testimonies. Researchers who study the grays often claim the aliens stare into their victim's eyes during abductions and that they can induce a hypnotic or hallucinogenic state in the abductee.

"Those eyes are hypnotic," recalled one abductee. *"They're black and opaque and there's no pupil there. I find myself staring into them and I can't move my body even though I want to. Somehow, through that eye contact, they are able to exert total control over my mind, and as a result, my body."*

In his book, *"Secret Life: Firsthand Accounts of UFO Abductions,"* author David Jacobs mentions the staring technique used by the gray aliens:

"Throughout the abduction, both as a way of communicating with the abductee and, presumably, of examining and altering her mental and emotional state, the beings stare deeply into the abductee's eyes."

If the aliens utilize this type of mind control, it could have many implications. Jacob's statement that it is used both for mental and emotional influence, gives us a hint of what these beings may be capable of. Furthermore, according to Jacobs, the technique *"extracts information from, or injects information into the abductee's head."*

Alien Human Hybrids

Beyond the dominant, large black eyes, and the unnatural, possibly artificial skin, there are other eerie similarities between the alien grays and the black eyed children. As David Jacobs and other researchers have noted, the gray aliens appear to communicate primarily though telepathic means. They also appear to utilize mind control techniques to some degree. While the black eyed children clearly communicate vocally, witnesses also claim the kids attempt to utilize telepathy or mind control in order to achieve their goals.

There are also certainly extreme differences between the grays and the BEKs. The grays usually appear with spindly bodies and long limbs. They are often described as 'fragile looking.' They do not have hair on their heads, nor do they attempt to wear human clothing, and most reports of the grays are directly related to UFO encounters. So, if the BEKs are not exactly grays, what, if any, is their connection to the so-called aliens?

A number of witnesses believe the black eyed children are a result of the gray aliens tampering with genetics, attempting to create alien/human hybrids. This theory proposes that the black eyed children are a result of experiments to blend alien and human DNA. The result, proponents believe, is a child with large 'alien' eyes, skin that resembles the gray aliens, and a limited amount of telepathic ability.

Hybrid History

The idea of alien-human hybrids is well known in the field of UFO studies. While many researchers discard it, believers point to early accounts that detail abductees having sperm and egg samples collected by aliens.

One of the most famous abduction cases, the Betty and Barney

Hill case, contains such details. The Hill's experience occurred in the fall of 1961 outside of Portsmouth, New Hampshire. It began on the night of September 19 when Betty and Barney Hill were driving back from a vacation in Niagara Falls. Traveling on an isolated road just south of Lancaster, New Hampshire, Betty spotted what she first thought was a falling star. The light acted erratically however, prompting Betty to convince her husband to stop the car at a picnic area.

Getting out of the car, the couple watched the lights for a brief time. Betty observed what she described as an 'odd shaped craft' traveling across the face of the moon. The craft flashed multicolored lights as it darted around in the night sky, moving closer to their position. Watching the craft rapidly descend in their direction, the couple quickly returned to the car and continued their journey. Barney drove toward Franconia Notch, a mountainous stretch of road.

Driving on the narrow, winding road, the Hill's kept their eyes on the strange, lighted craft. It kept pace with Betty and Barney's car, following it on the twisting road. The Hill's later stated the object seemed to be playing a cat and mouse game with them.

Approximately one mile south of Indian Head, New Hampshire, the object descended toward their vehicle, causing Barney to come to a stop in the middle of the highway. The Hill's observed the craft and its humanoid figures as it hovered over their car. Barney believed one of the UFO's occupants communicated with him on a telepathic level telling him; 'Stay where you are and keep looking.' In a later report to UFO investigator Walter Webb, Barney related that the "beings were somehow not human."

Coming out of the craft, a group of creatures took Betty and Barney out of their car and dragged them to a nearby clearing.

The next thing the Hill's knew, they were driving on the street that led to their home. It seemed the couple had lost four hours of time during the night's events. Although Betty could recall the strange lights and the 'little men' who dragged them from their car and to the clearing, her memories stopped after that.

The story of the Hill's encounter is considered the first modern alien abduction story. The full details of their encounter unfolded over time through work with a regression specialist. Hypnotic sessions revealed what had happened to the couple during the four hours they lost on the lonely New Hampshire road. Under hypnotic trance,

Barney recalled having a cup-like device placed over his genitals. The creatures apparently used the device to extract a sperm sample from Barney. This, the couple believed, was the reason Barney developed welts and pain in his genital area after the encounter.

As for Betty, she had her own memories of being examined by the strange beings. Betty recalled that a long, thin tube was inserted into her stomach, through her belly button. While this was an unknown process in 1961, obstetricians began to use it years later for in-vitro fertilization.

Were the Hill's test subjects for an alien hybridization project? Although theirs was the first widely publicized case, countless abductees since then have recounted similar stories. Many people now believe the gray aliens are using human DNA to create alien/human hybrids.

In *"The Everything UFO Book"* author William J. Birnes comments on the human/alien hybrid concept:

"If the alien hybrid theorists are correct, then successive generations of human children displaying increasing enhanced mental, telepathic, and athletic abilities might not be the results of normal evolution but enhanced evolution spurred by an extraterrestrial eugenics program."

While it may seem far out, this represents a fascinating possibility regarding the growing numbers of encounters with black eyed beings. Perhaps they are indeed the children of alien/human genes.

One woman certainly believes this to be the case.

Marcia's Account

Marcia J. of Wisconsin is convinced the black eyed children who showed up at her door are part of the alien hybridization program. She is confident in her opinion because she believes she has been abducted by gray aliens and has detailed memories of the experiences.

"I've been abducted numerous times since I was a child," she said.

"When I was twenty-three, the grays took eggs from me. I somehow 'knew' what they were going to do. During a later abduction, I was shown a small child. It had pale skin and large, solid black eyes. Once again I 'knew'

that this child had come from my genes."

"The grays communicate on a telepathic level. I was able to understand many of the things that I experienced during abductions because they put the information in my mind."

Marcia, who was thirty-four during the interview, claimed the black eyed children showed up on her doorstep ten years after she saw the child she believed was hers.

"I don't recall having any abduction experiences after I turned thirty. I'm still not sure why they stopped. Part of me was relieved and another part of me was sad. I thought about it less and less as time went by though.

One day, just after I had come home from work, I heard a knock on the back door. I had just sat my purse and keys down on the counter. We have double French doors that go out to a patio on the back of the house, just off the living room. I was standing there wondering who was knocking on those doors. At first, I was thinking it was my husband but that didn't make any sense. There's no way for him to lock himself out if he went out through those doors and the front door was unlocked when I had come in, he could have walked around. A little irritated, I walked over to the doors and pushed aside the curtain that covers the glass panels. Standing there, staring in the door at me, was a young boy about ten years old. He had pale skin, light sandy-colored hair and solid black eyes. Right away, I felt like I was in some kind of an altered state. I just sort of froze. He was standing very close to the glass, so I could see his features really well. I felt like he wanted to say something to me but his mouth didn't move. He just gazed back at me through the window. I don't even remember thinking about it, but I unlatched the lock and opened the door. I couldn't break eye contact with him; there was something so intense about him. When I opened the door, I could see that standing a few feet behind him was another boy. From what I could tell, he looked very, very similar to the one in front of me but his hair looked darker.

Suddenly, the front door of my house opened and my husband walked in saying very loudly, "Hi honey." My head spun around to look at him. He was walking across the room, asking me what I was doing. I snapped my head back around to the French doors. There was no sign of those boys."

Marcia says she pointed out to the patio, unable to say anything. Her husband, thinking something was wrong, walked out onto the patio but didn't see anyone or find any signs of trouble.

The couple lived in a community with very small yards with neighbors on each side. There is a fence at the back of the property, so anyone leaving would have to go through a locked gate, or climb the wooden fence. The only other exit lies along the left side of the house, toward the front yard, but Marcia's husband had blocked it that day with work equipment. The children Marcia witnessed standing on her back patio had vanished. When her husband came back inside, he found Marcia sitting on the sofa, crying.

"I felt dizzy and light-headed," she recalled. *"I couldn't stop crying. I was sad and happy at the same time, a real mix of emotions because I knew that I had just seen my child and that he had been raised by the gray aliens."*

Marcia fully believes her hybrid son turned up at her house that evening to make contact, and to let her know he was 'out there.'

"I don't really expect to see him anymore, but I know that he's living out there among us and that he's growing into an amazing being."

Marcia believes the solid black eyes are a result of the hybrid process and that the appearance has some connection to the gray alien's home world.

"I do believe that those are their eyes. They're just really different from us and for some reason, their eyes need to look that way for them to see. The boy I saw had those same, large, black eyes just like the aliens. His skin was also pale with a grayish tint to it. From what I saw, it looked very smooth."

While Marcia's story may be difficult for some people to swallow, she is not alone in her belief that she has been used by aliens to breed hybrid beings. Another abductee, Ann, talks about the hybrid child she believes is a result of her pregnancy.

Ann's account

Ann is another woman who says she's been abducted multiple times. She claims she was physically pregnant for several months until she was abducted, for the third time, by aliens. After the third abduction, the fetus was gone, and there were no signs of her having been pregnant at all.

"I know that they placed that fetus in me to begin with. I don't understand it all, but I know that's what they did. I carried that baby for several months until that night when the grays took me again. The next day, my baby was gone."

This was not the end of Ann's story, however. Three years later, during yet another abduction, a child was brought out and shown to her while she was aboard the alien ship.

"He looked normal at first, a little thin, but healthy I thought. Then I noticed his eyes. They were solid black just like the aliens. I knew the boy was my baby; I had no doubt at all. I spoke to him but I don't remember him answering. He just smiled at me. I touched his hair, it was very fine but not like baby hair, it was more like hair on someone having chemo treatments, like it was all going to fall out. I touched his hand and it was kind of cold and it felt funny, like the skin was too mushy or something."

The aliens returned Ann to her house and the next day she had full memory of the events from the night before.

"That child could walk around in this neighborhood and people wouldn't realize anything was different until he got closer to them. Those eyes stand out and his skin was so clean, no freckles like I have."

After further reflection, Ann doesn't think her 'son' was completely healthy. She believes the aliens are experimenting with hybrids but don't have the process down yet.

"I don't think they've learned how to do it yet, at least not to perfection. If they have, some of these hybrids could be wandering around our cities right now and we probably wouldn't know. All they would have to do is hide their eyes with sunglasses or something."

Ann's story is not a unique one. Around the world, there are thousands of women who claim similar experiences. These women often have their fetuses taken from them in the early stages of their pregnancy. Much later, they are shown a hybrid child with black eyes and pale skin and they are told, usually through telepathy, that the child is theirs.

Alien Plots

Why would an alien race want, or need, to create hybrid beings? There are many proposed theories to explain why such an experiment may be taking place. These theories range from a dying race that needs an injection of fresh DNA in order to survive, to alien time travelers attempting to correct a mistake made in their past (which is our present).

An even more sinister theory that has followers postulates that the grays are attempting to take over our world by slowly breeding us out and phasing in beings with alien DNA. Over time, the human race will fade away to be replaced by the 'superior' DNA of the gray aliens, or so adherents say. A long-term strategy for conquering a world, to say the least. It would seem more prudent for the aliens to sit back and wait for humankind to destroy itself, as the odds of success seem better. If it all sounds like a grand science fiction adventure, it just may be, but on the other hand, there are endless numbers of people having encounters with gray aliens and with black eyed children. If these two groups are connected, perhaps there is something to be genuinely concerned about.

Is it a coincidence that many abductees describe alien-human hybrid children and that they resemble kids described in BEK reports? Off color, or unnatural skin, and large, solid black eyes are only the obvious surface traits. If the black eyed children have alien genes, they may share other, less obvious connections. Abilities such as telepathy and/or mind control may be natural for the BEKs, and large numbers of people who encounter the grays report the aliens do not speak physically.

Barney Hill mentioned telepathy in connection to his abduction experience, saying that the alien being communicated to him without speaking and told him to "Stay where you are and keep looking." If the grays are indeed creating hybrid beings, they could potentially have some degree of similar telepathic ability. Numerous black eyed children encounters report varying levels of 'mind control' or rather, attempted mind control. It is a disturbing prospect, but perhaps the black eyed children are actually alien/human hybrids who are out testing their skills and developing and perfecting their mind control tactics.

Jim's Story

Jim, in Baltimore, Maryland, believes the black eyed kids he ran into were alien beings.

"They didn't look natural to me at all. The eyes were creepy, yes, but combined with the pasty color of their skin, it was a sight that I just won't forget."

Jim said the children looked like the aliens he's seen on book covers and in movies.

"My brother was really into all the UFO stuff for awhile. He'd had a sighting, just a light in the sky really, but it did some strange things, and it got him interested. He was reading all kinds of books and magazines about aliens and UFOs. I was never personally interested enough to read the material, but I'd watch the movies with him sometimes. These kids, they sort of looked like those aliens on my brother's magazines and books. A bit spindly in build, big, big black eyes and ugly colored skin. They looked like they were sick to me. These kids had hair though, both of them had light-colored hair, one was very blonde and the other's a light brown."

Jim recalls the boys trying to hold his attention and lock eyes with him. He believed the kids were trying to exert some kind of psychic influence and control of his thoughts.

"They kept staring at me and I knew they wanted me to maintain eye contact. I didn't want to though. The eyes creeped me out. As I stood there, I kept feeling like the back of my head was itching or something, it was a weird feeling and I can't really describe what it was all about. Those boys just kept talking and I started hearing a buzzing noise like a bunch of bees swarming around me, but there was nothing there. I got out of there and didn't even look back at those kids. Good riddance to them."

Jim had long conversations with his brother, a UFO aficionado, about the black eyed boys.

"My brother is convinced they were aliens. He showed me all kinds of paintings that people had done based on their own experiences. When he showed me a picture of what was called an alien hybrid, I told him that's it.

That's what those boys looked like."

While Jim believes the boys may have tried to exert mental control over him. He also feels they were using a device to do so.

"I didn't see anything, but that buzzing noise, the more I thought about it, the more I thought that it could be some kind of a machine. It sounded electronic to me. I don't know. Maybe I just can't come to terms with a couple of kids having some kind of mental power that affected me that way."

Perhaps the aliens are using children, or at least what appear to be children, because kids are usually ignored by adults going about their daily business. A less noticed child, or child form, could pick and choose targets at will with little interference. Since the gray aliens themselves are usually reported as being between four and five feet tall, these 'children' could be much older than most people perceive.

One other possibility regarding mind control abilities and the grays is that most, or all, of the encounters are illusions. If the gray aliens, assuming they're real, do have telepathic abilities and can exert influence over the human mind, then perhaps they are programming their victims to 'see' exactly what they want them to; in other words -strange young children attempting to interact with humans.

The grays, with their supposed higher level of intelligence, may be running a grand psychology experiment here on Earth. Present a helpless child who is not quite human, and have them make a request for food, water or warmth, then see how people react. Perhaps it's a way to numb the populace to the idea of alien beings and weird encounters.

Other people propose the black eyed children are not illusions, but are physical beings—not hybrids though, rather, simply gray aliens in disguise. Using their mind controlling influence, perhaps the grays impress the image of a child upon the mind of their victims. The fight or flight reactions people experience may be the result of a 'crack' in the illusion, or a weakening of the mind control.

None of these possibilities may be as fascinating as the prospect of alien-human hybrids of course, but the concept brings up numerous questions.

Hybrid Science

Are these aliens really from another planet, perhaps another solar system altogether? Are they breeding us like animals and experimenting at will for scientific research, or are they studying our characteristics to ultimately take control of Earth?

While it is fascinating to speculate about hybrids, one burning question remains, are alien-human hybrids even possible? Expert opinions are divided, but one thing is clear, there would have to be a considerable amount of similarities between the two races for hybrids to be viable. Even races close in genetic makeup often produce sterile offspring when they are crossbred. If we are to believe the large number of abductees, then the aliens do appear to have biology that is at least similar to ours. Without specific information as to the genetic makeup of alien beings, we can't really answer the question sufficiently.

Of course, there is always the possibility the aliens have developed a way to compensate for any genetic differences. Perhaps that's what the black eyed children are really all about. If we consider the numerous experiences with black eyed kids in accounts received from abductees, the total number of encounters with black eyed beings rises dramatically and seems more significant.

Certain aspects are conspicuously absent in these cases, however. The strange demands to be invited inside, the foul odors and the extreme fear reactions induced in BEK witnesses is not present in alien-human hybrid encounters. If anything, many of the alien hybrid encounters give people a sense of peace and resolve about their personal abduction memories. While many abductees consider their experiences terrifying and horrible, a portion of them believe they have done something good to help another race that is somehow related to us.

The possibilities remain, the strange children with both human and alien features and abilities may represent the last hope for a dying race, or they may signal the end of ours.

Chapter 7

Men In Black

In the annals of UFO legend and lore there are tales of mysterious MIB, or Men in Black. These odd-behaving men appear on the doorsteps of those who have had encounters with unidentified flying objects. They intimidate and harass witnesses, often issuing veiled threats and warnings, cautioning witnesses not to speak to anyone about their UFO encounter.

There are various descriptions, or perhaps they're simply different versions of the Men in Black. They are usually dressed in black suits and wear black hats. They also wear dark sunglasses regardless of the time of day or night. Their skin is usually olive-toned or pale white with an odd, plastic-like sheen.

Theories to explain the Men in Black range from secret government agents to aliens, or alien-human hybrids to robots, and a myriad of other possibilities.. Many people assume the Men in Black are actually agents of the federal government, and some of the encounters indicate this may be the case, at least on occasion. But this may simply be a case of government, or non-government agencies, using the mythical power of the MIB to their benefit.

Certainly the government has been known to track people with an interest in UFOs, and it's likely some of them have been paid a visit by genuine agents of the federal government. Many people who have been harangued by the Men in Black also believe their phones are tapped. The government certainly can monitor phone calls if it chooses to do so.

Other witnesses believe the MIB aren't even remotely human. They cite the strange behavior, awkward use of language, and robotic-like actions of the men as proof of otherworldly origins. Historic accounts of encounters with Men in Black have created further speculation and added to the mystery of the MIB.

Beginnings of the Men in Black

The earliest report of an encounter with the Men in Black dates back to the early 1950's and involved a man named Albert Bender. Bender was a UFOlogist and founder of an organization formed to investigate the flying saucer mystery. His group, The International Flying Saucer Bureau, or, IFSB, was one of the earliest independent organizations to study UFOs. Formed in April 1952, the IFSB's membership grew quickly and within months, it had branches in other countries, an investigation unit, and a magazine called *"Space Review."* Despite its sudden growth and popularity, the organization still only lasted a year and a half, shutting down in October 1953. The mystery of the organization's sudden end is attributed to the founder's strange encounter with three Men in Black.

IFSB founder Albert Bender told friends in September 1953 that a trio of Men in Black had paid him a visit. Bender first claimed the three men identified themselves as government agents. Later versions of his story are even more vague as to the exact origins of the men. Bender further claimed the MIB gave him information about the true secret of unidentified flying objects, and that the information was frightening. Bender received a stern warning not to talk any further about UFOs. The following month, he wrote in Space Review:

"The mystery of the flying saucers is no longer a mystery. The source is already known, but any information about this is being withheld by order from a higher source."

Terrified by his encounter with the Men in Black and the information he was given about flying saucers, Bender promptly closed down the IFSB. He claimed the Men in Black had threatened him with prison if he continued his pursuit of information about UFOs, and he urged anyone interested in the flying saucer mystery to "Please be very cautious" when studying the subject.

The story gained attention on a large scale a few years later, thanks to one of the people Bender confided in. Gray Barker, a friend of Bender's, and a member of the IFSB, published a book that contained Bender's account of his run in with the Men in Black.

"They Knew Too Much About Flying Saucers," was a hit in 1956 and brought worldwide attention to the mystery of the IFSB's abrupt end, Albert K. Bender's encounter with the mysterious men, and Barker's book placed the MIB solidly in the mix of UFO legends. Barker referred to the Men in Black as 'enforcers' for a sinister 'silence group' with its own agenda involving UFOs. Anyone foolish enough to pursue the study of flying saucers was likely to receive a visit from these dark men if they got too close to the truth. Barker even speculated that the Men in Black weren't human at all but agents of some otherworldly organization.

This idea was given more fuel in 1962 when Albert Bender wrote his own book about the encounter, *"Flying Saucers and the Three Men."* In it, Bender claimed the three men who visited him on that night in 1953 weren't human at all, but monstrous representatives of an alien race from a distant planet called Kazik. They were on our planet to monitor information about flying saucers and to track anyone interested in the subject. The entire episode could be considered completely outrageous but for the fact that numerous other UFO witnesses have encountered strange Men in Black over the years.

Fortean researcher John Keel is one of those witnesses.

John Keel and the MIB

John Keel, best known for his book, *"The Mothman Prophecies,"* is the writer responsible for coining the term 'MIB,' short for Men in Black.

In 1967, Keel wrote an article for Saga magazine entitled, *"UFO Agents of Terror."* Through this article and subsequent work, Keel drew the conclusion that the Men In Black were agents of some supernatural force linked to other concepts such as demons, ghosts, and cryptozoological creatures like Mothman. He described the MIB as pale and bug-eyed with oriental features. According to Keel, they wore dark suits, turtleneck sweaters and exhibited very odd behavior.

John Keel himself encountered the Men In Black on more than

one occasion. In the summer of 1967, Keel received a series of weird phone messages. The voice on the other end of the phone told Keel to go by himself to a location on Long Island. Intrigued, Keel arrived at the designated location at the appointed time.

"I found a large black Cadillac containing two dark-skinned men in dark suits apparently waiting for me", Keel wrote.

The investigator recounts that the men blinked their headlights at him and then drove away slowly. He followed the car for several miles until the Cadillac vanished around a bend. Keel drove around for several minutes, attempting to find the car when suddenly it reappeared behind him. He pulled over and exited his car only to witness the Cadillac with the two strange men drive slowly by him. Keel believed the entire incident was staged to give him evidence that the Men In Black really did exist.

Modern Men In Black

The Men in Black often appear or disappear suddenly. They tend to use outdated slang terms and their language is both awkward and insistent. They stress that the witness must believe what they are saying and must follow their directive to remain silent about their UFO encounters.

The MIB often enter the homes of those they are harassing. Witnesses later feel puzzled as to why they let the men enter, leading some to believe the MIB are capable of mind control or hypnosis. Strangely, the MIB often have detailed information about the people they confront, implying the person has been under surveillance for some time. Common, everyday items seem to puzzle the MIB. They have exhibited confusion over such things as pens, forks and Jell-O.

Strange electronic phenomena are associated with the Men in Black too. Odd noises and robotic voices on telephones, electronic beeping noises, static or other interference when attempting to make calls may all occur prior to or after an encounter with the MIB.

Author and researcher of the strange, Nick Redfern penned an excellent book on the MIB, titled, *"The Real Men In Black."* After the book was released, Redfern had a personal experience with strange electronic phenomena. Appearing for a radio interview, Redfern discussed the Men in Black and some of the odd things associated with them. In Redfern's words:

"When we got to the section of the interview about telephone interference.... all hell broke loose."

Static, strange noises and interference manifested in the middle of the interview. When asked his opinion regarding the strange sounds, Redfern responded to the interviewer:

"I told her, in my opinion, if this was not a case of coincidence (and the timing most strongly suggests it was not!) Then maybe someone really was listening in and playing a few mind-games of the MIB variety."

Despite having written a book on the Men in Black, Redfern never experienced such phenomena himself until that point. Perhaps the Men in Black wanted to prove their existence to him as they had done with John Keel many years previously.

Devils and the MIB

John Keel and other researchers have pointed to interesting parallels between modern Men in Black and historic accounts of encounters with the devil, who often appeared as a well-dressed man in a black suit. Keel himself believed the MIB were a modern manifestation of some demonic force once interpreted as the devil or perhaps beings of the fairie realm. Indeed, the term 'the black man' was used for centuries to refer to the devil, not because of his skin color, but due to his chosen attire.

As the years moved forward, this same dark force continued to manifest to people in various forms. The popularity of UFO studies and the flying saucer craze of the '50s and '60s helped co-create the strange flying-saucer-connected version of the Men in Black.

Folklorist Thomas E. Bullard is a specialist in UFO-related mysteries. In his text *"UFO Abductions: The Measure of a Mystery"* he writes about the Men in Black and their place in the larger scope of the mythology of strange visitors:

"Almost a sense of familiarity attaches to the Men in Black. They step into the shoes vacated by angels and demons to serve as modernized versions of otherworldly messengers, modified to reflect extraterrestrial rather than supernatural employment but clearly functionaries in the same mold."

Bullard looks at the MIB in comparison to other beings perceived as messengers of divine powers. He continues:

"Even high gods like Odin in Norse mythology sometimes disguised themselves and roamed the earth to dispense justice or stir up strife among humans, but this sort of work usually devolved on a servant class of beings."

A further statement from Bullard:

"Devils and demonic beings enjoy broader license for mischief as they cause harm by whatever means their evil imaginations can devise."

Interesting enough, these statements could easily apply to the black eyed children. Are they the latest version of Men in Black type messengers, sent by some higher power to cause strife and disruption? Perhaps the classic image of the MIB became too tame for some situations and a higher force created the black eyed children in order to grab the attention of a jaded, overwhelmed public tired of old stereotypes.

Chapter 8

Hungry Ghosts

"The black eyed children are spirits from the realm of the hungry ghost," professes Jill, a woman of Chinese descent now living in America. Jill's sister had an encounter with one of the black eyed kids in China, and she considers herself lucky to have escaped the spirit's evil glare.

"My sister saw one of the black eyed children at our parent's home in China; it was many years ago. The spirit was a little girl, maybe eight years old, and she said she wanted food, she wanted to come inside to eat. This is what the hungry ghosts do; they always want something, but they can never be satisfied because they are stuck in a realm between worlds. If you let them in, great misfortune will fall on you and your family."

Hungry Ghost Traditions

The concept of the hungry ghost realm is well integrated into Chinese culture. In fact, there is an annual celebration called the "Hungry Ghost Festival." The festival is held every year during the seventh month of the Chinese calendar, during the full moon. According to tradition, the gates of hell are open during this time and the hungry ghosts are free to roam the land. The spirits wander about looking for food, entertainment, and anything else that will fulfill their desires.

To appease the spirits, families offer prayers to their deceased relatives. People also pay tribute to any unknown wandering spirits who may be roaming about. It is believed such 'homeless' spirits, or those with no family remaining on earth, can cause great misfortune if they are not honored.

Public celebrations are held to entertain the hungry ghosts. Seats in the front rows are left empty so the spirits have a place of honor to sit. Food is prepared and left out on altars to feed the wandering spirits. It is considered unacceptable and even dangerous for the living to sit in seats reserved for the spirits or to eat food from the portions left out for them. Celebrants burn joss paper, a thin tissue-like paper, with pictures of houses, cars and other objects of desire. They also burn large quantities of 'hell money.' Printed on joss paper to resemble paper money, hell money is considered valid currency in the underworld and by burning it, hungry ghosts are given the currency to use as they wish in the afterlife.

Jill's Account

Jill shared the story of her sister's encounter with a black eyed ghost:

"She came home from the market one day; she still lived with our parents in Shanghai. She made some tea and was doing things in the kitchen, preparing food for dinner. There was a knock at the window of the kitchen and she looked over to see a girl standing there outside. It was warm and the window was half opened to let the air in. My sister walked over to the window and looked at the girl. Right away, she saw that the little girl had black eyes and that her skin was very white and pale. My sister asked the girl what she wanted and the girl told her:

'I want to eat. I want you to invite me in so I can have some of your food.'

My sister was very afraid. She thought the girl was some kind of spirit. She told me the girl looked strange and didn't appear completely solid. She was not far away from the window and the girl was staring straight at her.

She left the kitchen and called out to our father who was resting. She told him about the girl and what she said. Father went into the kitchen but there was no sign of the little girl. He closed the window and the curtains and then said they should all do prayers because my sister had seen a wandering spirit."

Jill's family spoke with both a Buddhist and a Taoist priest. The house was blessed and rituals were done to cleanse the home, the family, and, to help the wandering spirit find peace. The family firmly believes that had the spirit been allowed into the home, great misfortune would have befallen them all.

"Sometimes people feel pity for these wandering spirits and they make the mistake of letting them in, but you have to appease them in the proper way. They don't know how to limit what they take and if you let them in, they will steal all of your good fortune away."

Jill says she has seen 'clouds of spirits' moving in the streets during the time of the hungry ghosts, but she has never encountered one of them the way her sister did.

"Every year, we still take precautions. It's not good to stay outside too long after dark because you might run into one of the spirits. We put food out for them, burn incense and joss, and pray for them. Even for the ones who aren't your ancestors, maybe they have no one to pray for them, so we honor them and hope they can move on to their next life. Sometimes, they are the most dangerous, because they will try to attach themselves to anyone.

I hope that I never come that close to one of the hungry ghosts like my sister did. Some of them just need help, but some of them are very evil."

History of the Hungry Ghosts

The concepts of hungry ghosts flow through much of Chinese culture and religious tradition. The realm of the hungry ghost itself is a frightening place, a mere single notch above the realm of hell itself. In general terms, it is believed that everyone becomes a ghost once they pass from the world of the living. Eventually a person's 'ghost' weakens and completely releases all ties to the physical world, then "dies" a second time before finally moving on to (hopefully) higher realms of the afterlife. Some spirits, however, become stuck in an in-between space and move into the realm of the hungry ghost. There are numerous reasons this may occur. One such cause is lack of veneration by the person's ancestors.

Honoring family members who have died is very important in Asian culture. It is both a sign of respect as well as a necessity to ensure the spirit can pass on to higher realms and not stay around to haunt the living. The primary reason one becomes trapped in the realm of the hungry ghost has to do with the life they led while they were living.

Negative behavior has a direct influence on the afterlife, and one's actions dictate what happens after death. Anger, greed, jealousy and ignorance are all factors that can cause someone to become a hungry ghost. It is a cursed existence with the spirit forever driven by intense desires. Although the cravings are strong, nothing can bring satisfaction, since these beings are not fully alive. Without bodies they cannot feel or appreciate things connected to the physical world, in spite of their desires.

The idea of hungry ghosts dates far back in Chinese history. When Buddhism entered China, it clashed with adherents of the Confucian tradition and other systems that practiced ancestor worship. Veneration of ancestors was a vital component of society's wellbeing, and it eventually merged into the Buddhist traditions of China. The Buddhists already had their own concept of the hungry ghost realm, and the two systems married together.

In China's Taoist religion, hungry ghosts are often the spirits of those who could not find the things they needed to survive in the afterlife. Taoists believe a ghost 'stuck' without the proper amount of food, water, and shelter will find its way back into the land of the living. In its desperation, the spirit will seek out humans and attempt to feed on their energy. This is often done by attempting to frighten a person, causing them to experience a spike in emotional energy, and feeding on the feelings invoked. The Taoists also believe a hungry ghost can result from violent or sudden deaths, or from people who died miserable and unhappy.

Taoist tradition teaches that the way in which a building is constructed and placed will determine whether a hungry ghost will be attracted to it. It is therefore vital to consult with an expert before undertaking building projects.

The Taoist tradition deals with hungry ghosts through rituals, prayers and chants. Food and other objects are offered to the spirit to help it survive. It is believed that by helping the spirit, it will be able to move out of the realm of hungry ghosts and transition into the next world.

Hungry ghosts and similar concepts are common throughout most of Asia. It is believed these spirits have gone beyond mere human suffering and are doomed to suffer extreme hunger, thirst and desire.

These were once living people, who because of their karma are now afflicted in the afterlife. Their insatiable desire is often for something repugnant or strange. No matter how bizarre an object or action, there is likely a hungry ghost craving it.

Other Wandering Spirits

In Tibet, the term for lost or wandering spirits is 'Yidak.' Sikh, Hindu and Jain texts also refer to these spirits, and the common name used is 'Preta,' a Sanskrit term. Preta is used to describe a supernatural being invisible to the human eye. It is thought that in certain mental states, humans can see these spirits.

Preta are described as having a human form with sunken gray skin. Sometimes they are depicted as being very mummy-like, with distended stomachs, a representation of their hunger. These spirits have enormous appetites and they can never be satiated.

In Japan, preta is roughly translated as 'gaki.' Interestingly, modern Japanese use the term gaki as slang to refer to a brat, spoiled child or young punk.

Do any of these spirits fit in with the so-called black eyed children? While it's clear there are many differences between hungry ghosts and the BEKs, it is interesting to consider the cultural interpretation of such beings and how they would be perceived in modern Asia. Contemporary accounts of black eyed children from Asia are few and far between. I have spoken to a number of Asian Americans who firmly believe such beings fall into the concept of the realm of hungry ghosts. It's likely that tales from Asia would find their way into modern ghost stories. Encounters, therefore, would probably be related in a fashion similar to Jill's story above.

The idea of a hungry ghost being driven by desire is also quite interesting when considered in conjunction with the BEKs. Many encounters with black eyed beings provoke fear, paranoia and intense emotional and even physical reactions. Some people feel drained for days after their exchanges with the BEKs. If these beings are like the hungry ghost, they may be feeding on the reactions of those to whom they appear. A hungry ghost attempting to produce an extreme emotional response could take lessons from black eyed kid encounters!

.

Chapter 9

The Devil You Say

One of the most common assumptions many people leap to regarding the BEKs is that they are demonic in nature. While it's true the children exhibit some characteristics similar to those of demonic entities, I believe there is also another factor to consider.

The pursuit of demons and the demonic are currently 'in vogue.' Over the last several years there's been a propensity in the paranormal field to find demons lurking around every corner. The trend is unfortunate for many reasons. It has led to countless, self-proclaimed 'Demonologists' doling out 'expert' opinions and advice about everything from BEKs to aliens and the Mothman.

The cold truth is there are very few reputable demonologists with proper training and experience in the field. It's easy enough to learn the basic, common beliefs regarding demons by putting in the time and energy to read and research, but you can't dart out and get a degree in demonology. Nor should anyone self-appoint themselves a 'demonologist.' To do so is to invite trouble.

While I don't discount the possibility that these strange children are dark in nature, I do not personally believe they are specifically (only) demons in the biblical sense. With that being said, it's time to play devil's advocate (you knew I had to say that), and offer up some of the reasons that this interpretation of the strange children may be a possibility, in accordance with standard religious beliefs regarding demons.

91

Whether the black eyed children are physical manifestations or not seems irrelevant in encounters with people of a religious background. The bottom line is, many witnesses believe they have had a brush with the demonic and they respond based on their religious beliefs. While demonic entities cross over into most orthodox religions, the concept most people are familiar with is the Christian one. In fact, the Catholic faith, has, at times in its history, employed 'exorcists' specifically trained to cast out or 'exorcise' demons.

The dictionary defines 'demon' as "an evil spirit or an agent of evil, harm, distress or ruin." The BEKs certainly seem to cause a great deal of distress when they appear. Many people feel an 'evil presence' about the children even though they have not perpetrated any evil acts that we are aware of or can confirm. There is no denying the number of people who feel disturbed by their encounters with the kids. Their presence is described as 'malevolent,' 'sinister' and 'frightening.' They seem to universally scare the people who encounter them. One witness stated, *"I felt like this kid was a predator and he was sizing me up. It was the most disturbing thing I've ever felt."*

These feelings seem to linger with the victims for some time after their encounters. Those who meet the BEKs have a very difficult time forgetting the experience, and often suffer sleepless nights, bad dreams and outright nightmares. Many witnesses report continued unease for days or even weeks after the encounter. One witness said, *"I kept thinking they were going to show up again. I couldn't go back to the area where I had encountered them; it was just too nerve-wracking."*

These kinds of reactions are identical to someone who has experienced a traumatic event. The results of an encounter with these children goes much deeper than the basic experience of seeing and interacting with them. It's doubtful normal kids could have such a deep impact on the average adult.

As to specific correlations between the black eyed children and demons, there are several.

First are the pure black eyes, which are often perceived as evil or sinister. Some accounts do indeed link the lack of eye color, or solid black eyes, to demonic forces. The belief is that the entity is so filled with evil or darkness that nothing else can come through the eyes, i.e., no "light." At the least, such an appearance is certainly unsettling for those who witness it. Would a demon intentionally manifest with pure black eyes? It seems unlikely since their goal is to lure people in and take them by surprise. Black eyes on pale skin shine like a beacon and it's not a trait that's easily hidden. What if the demon didn't have any choice though? According to demonology experts, a demon can take human form only if some part of the body remains demonic. Often, it's a foot or hand that remains distorted and demonic in structure, while the rest of the body adapts to a normal human appearance. Demons, in fact, are purported to be able to take on very attractive forms to catch their victims unaware. This makes sense in terms of demonic lore and the supposed goals of sinister beings.

Unless we count the eyes and pale skin, demonic body parts are not in evidence in BEK reports. This does not mean all the limbs are intact and normal by human standards. In fact, usually, witnesses have a hard time remembering details about the hands or feet of the children. Once fixated on the strange eyes, it seems other details become difficult to notice or remember. Could it be the coal black eyes are the evil mark required by demonic entities? If the entity left its eyes black intentionally, it is perhaps not the wisest choice.

One might wonder why a demon would choose the form of a child, but the explanation is simple. The form of a child is much more appealing than a six-foot, black-eyed man. There's something about a child that immediately causes most people to let their guard down. The prospect of a child being in trouble or need, invokes the natural protection instinct most adults feel towards children.

It's difficult for an adult to feel threatened by a child. Perhaps it is a primal instinct that says children must be cared for. When a child is suddenly in the role of the one posing a danger, a shift in basic belief must take place. This may be one of the reasons that people who encounter these dark eyed children have such a difficult time comprehending what is happening to them. Countless reports include witnesses wrestling with this very concept, trying to understand why a young child seems so sinister.

This, of course, would play right into the plan of a demonic entity. Present an image that couldn't possibly be threatening and use it to catch the victim off guard. While the witness is busy trying to help a "child" who needs to come in for some water, the demon has gained an invitation across the threshold. Many religious traditions believe an evil spirit cannot enter a household without receiving an invitation.

These children are certainly persistent in attempting to enter homes, buildings and even cars. In many reports, the BEKs act surprised when the victim does not give in to their request. Often in encounters they seem to become angry when their victims don't simply open their doors and make way for them to enter.

Not only do these kids radiate a sinister attitude, they are very elusive when presented with direct questions. Perhaps they simply don't know how to respond when questioned about their strange requests. Their usual tactic is to repeat the request they made to begin with. Try to pin them down about the whys of their needs and they don't appear to have an answer.

Another trait that occurs in some BEK encounters is a foul odor. This odor is not always noticed during the encounter but is often apparent after the children have vanished. It's described as a 'sickly sweet' or sometimes 'rotten egg' smell. Other people have likened it to the scent of something decaying, or of rotting garbage. Interestingly, the rotten egg smell is often how people describe sulfur, a substance usually associated with demonic entities and the forces of the underworld.

BEKs in Toronto

John was working overnight security for an office building in Toronto. He worked in security for several years and he liked the graveyard shift because it was always quiet. He would walk his rounds, and in between, sit and read at the front desk. John always brought a pile of magazines with him because they were easy to read in short snippets.

It was late at night on a Thursday in 2007 when he heard a rapping sound on the glass at the building's main entrance. Approaching the front, John noticed two kids standing at the glass doors. One of them was rapping on the glass, long and steady. Even though they must have seen the guard approaching the door, the kid continued to knock on the glass. The two boys wore hooded sweatshirts and were standing very close to the glass. He could see the boys very clearly, and estimated them to be in their early teens. John felt a chill come over him when he reached the glass door. The boy looked directly at John, putting his face close to the glass.

"Let us in," the boy said.

John spoke out loudly. *"Office is closed boys; you'll have to come back tomorrow."*

"Let us in," the boy repeated.

John looked closer at the boys, wondering why they were out so late at night. The neighborhood was fairly safe, and in all his time as a guard for the building, John had rarely had any incidents. Occasionally a drunk or homeless person would show up trying to get in or use the bathroom. They usually went on their way when the guard appeared.

The boys continued to stare in through the glass door. They were clearly visible in the building's entrance lights and John now realized what was 'wrong' about the situation. The boy staring at him had solid black eyes. The guard swallowed hard and tried to take a deep breath to calm his nerves. Before he could respond, the boy spoke again.

"Let us in. We want to read your magazines."

John thought perhaps the kids were on drugs, or attempting to play a prank, or perhaps both. He held up a portable phone he had grabbed off the desk and made a point of letting the kids see it. A thought then struck him. How did the kids know he had magazines? They were in a pile on the desk and not visible from the entrance. Was it a lucky guess? It made him feel even more uneasy. He tried his best to stay calm but his nerves were on edge.

"Look boys, just go home. You can't hang around here. I'll call the cops if I need to."

The boy was still rapping on the glass and the noise was starting to get on the guard's nerves.

"Let us in so we can see your magazines."

John couldn't answer. He looked at the strange boy and then at his phone. He looked down, dialed the number for the police station and put the phone to his ear, looking up as he did so.

The boys were gone. In those few seconds, they had vanished.

John was quickly against the glass, looking in each direction, trying to catch a glimpse of which way the boys had gone. There wasn't anything nearby that would offer a hiding place for the kids. How could they have vanished so quickly? They must have taken off at a dead run, he thought.

John quickly disconnected the call. Maybe he was tired and his mind was playing tricks on him. He stood there for a moment trying to process what had happened. Convinced he couldn't have imagined the boys, he opened the door to have a look around the entrance. He wanted to make sure they weren't hanging around outside where he couldn't see them. When he pulled open the door, a foul odor overwhelmed him. The stench was so bad John felt his stomach heave. He covered his mouth and nose with the side of his jacket, fighting the urge to vomit. He had never smelled anything like it before. He closed the door quickly and stepped back several feet. Going back toward the entrance, he found that the odor still lingered in the entire entrance area. John covered his nose again and went outside. The foul smell was all around the door where the kids had been standing. He took several paces in each direction, scanning the street and sidewalk to see if there was any sign of the kids. Finding nothing, he went back into the building.

The smell lingered around the front entrance for a good hour or more. John describes it as 'rotten eggs and fecal matter mixed together.' *"It was the worst odor I've ever encountered,"* he said. *"For days, I felt like that smell was on my clothes. I washed my uniform three times and still thought that I could smell it."*

Is this horrible scent a result of the black eyed children being demonic in nature? Foul odors are often associated with demons. If these beings are truly something from the depths of hell, it would make sense they would bear the stench of the underworld. Demonic entities are often associated specifically with the smell of sulfur which some people describe as a 'rotten egg' odor.

Vampiric Beings

Demons pulled straight from the pit of hell aren't the only evil entity the black eyed children share traits with. There are commonalities with another classic creature of the darkness, the vampire.

According to classical tales of vampires, the bloodsuckers supposedly have an awful smell, reflective of the belief they have recently crawled from the grave. Like demons, the foul stench of vampires is overwhelming. While the modern image of the vampire has become romantic and sexy, earlier tales reflect the concept that they were beings of the underworld, brought to life by a curse or black magic.

In classical tales, vampires are unable to bear the light of the sun or the power of holy places. The need for human blood drives them and they must return to their coffins each day.

Other tales of the undead report a 'sickly sweet' smell associated with them. This is often viewed as a result of the magical forces that created the vampire, or their consumption of blood, which has a distinct odor.

Janet encountered a BEK in the parking lot of a Walmart in Virginia:

"I had arrived at the Walmart and parked my car. It wasn't very busy and there were no other cars parked on either side of mine. I reached over to the passenger floor and got my purse. When I turned to open my door, there was this boy standing there. It gave me a real start. My window was partially cracked and he put his mouth near the opening."

"I want a ride," the boy said.

"I felt the hair go up on the back of my neck. Before I even said anything, he repeated the same thing again. Then I noticed a strong odor. I don't know how to describe it except as a sickeningly sweet smell. It made me feel queasy.

I started the car back up and put it in gear. The boy took a step back and I saw his eyes. They were a solid, shiny black. I sped away without looking back. I just wanted to get home and lock my doors.

That smell stayed in the car. In fact, the further I drove away from that boy, the worse the smell seemed to get. I rolled the windows down to air the car out. Even when I got home, it still lingered in the car some. That boy gave me the creeps so bad; I know he was of the devil. I wouldn't go back to that Walmart without my husband after that. Even with him there, I still look around the lot good before I get out of the car."

Classical vampire lore recounts that the undead cannot enter a dwelling unless invited in. They can come to the threshold, but not cross it until the invitation is given. One of the primary requests that come up in most BEK encounters is the desire to be invited in. To date, there have been no cases reported wherein a BEK has forcefully violated a person's house, vehicle or other space. Even when there was opportunity the children have not forced their way inside. Is this because the invitation was not given? Are these beings limited in some way, like a vampire?

This clear correlation with vampire lore is interesting, but there is yet another trait shared by the two. Classic vampire stories say the bloodsucker can exert hypnotic influence on victims. Often this is done by making eye contact or having the victim gaze into an object such as a ring or necklace. Calm, rhythmic speech is used to lull the person's mind into a state of compliance. Since vampires are able to charm their victims, is this what the black eyed children are attempting? If so, it would appear they have not yet perfected the technique. Adults who have encountered these attempts come close to complying, but have been able to 'break the spell' of the BEKs. These attempted hypnotic suggestions are usually done by repeating the same phrases over and over in a monotone voice.

"Just let us in."

"You don't have to think about it."

"This won't take long."

Like the vampires of legend, the BEKs are attempting to compel their victims into doing what they would not normally consider. Although the children attempt to act proper and polite, their behavior causes a great deal of unease. Many people who have had close encounters with the beings report a malevolent or predatory energy, as though the kids are 'hunters.' Again, this is in keeping with dark tales of vampires hunting their human prey.

Witnesses who have encountered the attempted mind control tactic report a 'foggy' feeling coming over them. They often consider giving in to the requests and they wrestle with the rational mind and their feelings of fear. It doesn't occur to them until after the encounter that the children tried to influence their minds and control their actions.

In reflection, most people feel the children wanted to enter for some sinister reason. Do these beings have some evil purpose they are trying to achieve? This type of behavior makes it easy for some people to assume the black eyed children are demonic in nature. Indeed, the very behavior of these kids reinforces the argument that they are dark in nature and have an evil intent. What is hard to determine is what it is they want. If they merely want entrance into a home, why have they not forced their way in? Is there really some energy or force that prevents them from entering without an invitation? Perhaps the invitation they seek is symbolic of being accepted in some way. That leads to another concept to explain the BEKs.

Spirits of Children

What if these beings are the spirits of deceased children? If so it represents a disturbing possibility, for it would seem to indicate these are spirits trapped on Earth. Certainly, the trends of the last twenty years have seen an unsettling change in youth. Stories of children killing other children and committing horrendous acts have been splashed across front pages around the world. If our physical reality is reflected in the spiritual world, perhaps some of these unsettled spirits continue to linger.

It is interesting to note that many young criminals are said to have 'empty or blank' eyes and devoid of emotion. What happens when these kids die? Do they cross over to face the karma of their actions, or do they remain stuck here by fate or by choice? Frightening images of children stick in the mind and are not easy to comprehend. It's one of the reasons Hollywood has had success with the use of kids in horror settings in films. There's something unnatural and unnerving that affects our psyche when presented with such stories.

Yet another possibility is the black eyed children are actual physical kids who have been possessed by a demon or other evil spirit. This prospect raises more questions than it answers, however. If these are indeed children who have been possessed, then where are they all hiding when they're not out knocking on doors? It would seem at least one of these possessed children would have turned up, or their families would have taken them somewhere for help. The average parent would take their child to a physician, or possibly a priest, right away if any strange traits were exhibited.

It is interesting to note, a large percentage of people who have run-ins with the BEKs find themselves drawn to a more spiritual or religious life because of the encounter. Disturbed at what they feel was an 'evil' being, they seek solace and comfort from a minister or other religious leader. Those who have encountered the kids come from a wide variety of belief systems, crossing many lines of spiritual thought and religious tradition, but their reactions are largely the same.

BEKs and the End Times

Some Christians who have encountered the black eyed children are believers in end time prophecies. They believe the BEKs are a sign of the devil and the coming end times prophesied in the Book of Revelations. Taken as another sign of the apocalypse, these Christians believe the BEKs are agents of evil and are sent to try to tempt Christ's followers away from their righteous path.

Sharon is an example of one such Christian. She lives in Raleigh, North Carolina and encountered the black eyed children in a local park. Her encounter led her to delve more deeply into her religious beliefs, and she feels the challenge presented by these 'demons' actually saved her from damnation. She believes the end times are rapidly approaching and by becoming more spiritual, she is on a path to salvation.

Sharon is in her mid-thirties and is happily married with two kids. She and her husband have attended a local church regularly for over ten years, and they never gave a thought to anything paranormal—at least, not until a fateful day at a local park. The couple had taken their two kids, ages seven and ten, out for a picnic on a Tuesday afternoon. They parked in the designated parking lot for the area and walked a short distance down a gentle slope to a spot they had used before. There was plenty of grass to sit on and an open area to play ball with the kids. The family spent about two hours at the park, playing with the kids and eating lunch. Finally, Sharon began to clean up, knowing they needed to get back home before rush hour. She gathered up the picnic items and told her husband she was taking them to the car while he played catch with the boys. She carried the items to the car and placed them inside. She closed the door, turned around, and was surprised to see two boys standing in the lot several feet away. They looked like twins between the ages of eight and ten. They were standing side-by-side staring at Sharon. She smiled and said hello but they didn't respond. Perhaps they were shy, she thought. She glanced around and realized there were no other cars in the parking lot.

"Did you boys get lost?" she asked.

There was still no response and Sharon felt an odd chill come over her. The boys had very dark eyes and she realized their clothing looked rather old and ill-fitting. Perhaps they were homeless children. Sharon turned and looked around the lot again and past her own car. When she turned back toward the kids, she found they were now much closer to her. How had they moved so quickly and quietly? She was around children all the time, but she had never felt so nervous before. She looked at the kids again. Now that they were closer, and she could see more details, Sharon realized the boys had black eyes. She'd never seen such a condition before. Finally, the boy on the left spoke to her.

"We want to ride in your car."

Sharon's unease grew at the tone of the boy's voice. It was monotone and demanding at the same time. She took a deep breath and responded.

"Do you boys need help?"

The two children continued to stare at her and the same boy responded.

"We want to come to your house."

The statement was short and cold. Sharon felt her sense of dread growing quickly. She turned and took a quick look down the slope, hoping her husband was coming to the car but she couldn't see him. When she turned back toward the boys, they had once again moved closer. Sharon's fear was growing to a panic. She backed up a few paces, keeping the children in sight this time.

"I'll get my husband. He's right over there, and then we'll try to help you."

When she had moved back several more steps, Sharon turned, almost running. She took a quick look back to see if the boys were following her but they were gone. Somehow, in those few seconds, they had completely vanished.

Sharon called for her husband. He rushed to her, boys in tow. In all their years together, he had never heard his wife in such a state. She quickly told him the story of the strange black eyed children. He searched the parking lot and the surrounding area but found no sign of the children anywhere. It seemed impossible that they could have disappeared so suddenly. Once she was home and had calmed down, Sharon discussed the event further with her husband. She believed she had encountered something demonic and she and her husband decided to contact their pastor. Since then, the three have had numerous conversations about the encounter. It continues to haunt Sharon. She believes she was confronted by something evil that took an innocent form to lure her in. In the days that followed, Sharon felt deeply concerned for her family. She says it took her days of prayer to feel safe and secure even in her own home. Although confident in her faith, Sharon never returned to the park where she had her encounter.

Religious believers are convinced the black eyed children are here to collect souls and steal the life force of anyone foolish enough to fall for their tricks. As agents of evil, the BEKs have no soul; hence, there is no color in their eyes. Their dark nature and their black eyes are merely a reflection of the emptiness within.

Whether or not the black eyed children have any connection to demonic forces, they have steered numerous people like Sharon to delve deeper into their personal spiritual paths. For these people, what they faced was demonic, or, at the very least, evil. These encounters challenged them to question the strength of their faith. For many, it caused them to correct their path and to conduct themselves in a more spiritual manner in accordance with their religious beliefs. Rather than 'capturing souls,' it seems the BEKs drive people away from the demonic and toward religion in these cases.

Perhaps the devil needs to reevaluate his tactics if he's hoping to gain followers in this fashion.

Chapter 10

Tricksters

A vast array of beings fall within the spectrum of the trickster archetype. Jesters and jokers, fools, and modern clowns. Shape shifters and sorcerers, elementals and even the infamous Men in Black. The trickster is neither good nor evil, managing to stay in a mystical gray area between the two.

In the Pacific Northwest, he is the Raven. In the southwest, he is known as Coyote. Reynard the Fox in France, Maui in Hawaii, Saci in Brazil, the list goes on and on. The trickster is an archetypal figure and as such, can be found in some form within mythologies around the world. At times, he plays the idiot, bringing transformation by sheer folly. In other forms, he is sinister and scheming, working to play one side against the other for his own enjoyment and goals.

The trickster has no moral code to follow, no values to promote. He is a messenger, a creator and a transformer. Following his impulses and spontaneous desires, he straddles the line between good and evil and thoroughly enjoys the position. His destructive nature raises awareness and offers opportunities to those ready and willing to change their lives. For those not prepared, his lessons are harsh.

Amid the turmoil he creates, the trickster remains unaffected by the chaos. In fact, he revels in it, using it as his driving force, his fuel as he runs amok outside the laws of nature.

The trickster is especially prominent among Native Americans where he often appears in animal form. The most well know of these is Coyote of the tribes of the Southwestern United States. The rich lore of this cultural hero has spread throughout the country but he is not the lone trickster in the Americas.

Africans brought their own trickster stories to the United States during the slave trade. In the Deep South, their stories blended with Native American tales and morphed into the character of Brer Rabbit, a central figure in the Uncle Remus stories famous in the American Deep South.

The trickster archetype continued to transform through the decades but never vanished. In later years, the trickster became the jester, which eventually evolved into the modern clown. Still bending the laws of what is acceptable and natural, the clown continues to be a catalyst that calls us to question how we view the world. The clown can perform the most sacred task in irreverent fashion and get away with it. He represents both the spiritual and the absurd at the same time.

Trickster Gods

There are trickster gods too. In Norse mythology, the god of fire and trickery is known as Loki. Loki is often portrayed as one of the more sinister tricksters. In traditional myths, he often creates dangerous situations, which the other gods, usually his brother Thor, must deal with. While many of these situations are created by his sheer folly, others are more malicious and intentional on his part. Loki revels in disobeying the normal laws of gods and nature, and his very abilities seem to reflect this. He is also the god of thieves and cunning. He is an adept shape-shifter able to change into numerous forms, and able to change his gender. Loki also has eyes that change color, turning red as fire or black as night.

Tricksters at the Door

Like the proverbial trickster, the black eyed children operate outside the laws we commonly accept as normal. They create trouble with each appearance and they seemingly appear and disappear at random. They cause disruptions on a mental and emotional level and they are credited with various abilities any trickster would be proud to utilize. For some time, it seemed stories of the black eyed children were confined to the United States. In recent years, however, international accounts have begun to surface. Encounters in countries as widespread as Canada, Australia and South Africa now indicate these strange children are expanding their presence, or maybe they were always there in the shadows.

Richard's Story

I was very intrigued by an encounter related to me by a government employee from London, England. It's the first account I received from the UK and the encounter contains interesting and unusual elements.

Richard M. of London recounts his tale of a strange visit by the black eyed children:

"After a long day, I left work and headed home. It was a Thursday evening. I live on the second floor of an older building, but it does have a keyed entry at the front so you have to live there to get in. I went in the main door and closed it behind me. The door locks automatically. I headed straight up the stairs to my flat.

I'd no sooner put my things down when I heard a loud thumping noise outside my door. I stood there for a moment, half expecting a knock to come but it didn't. I thought perhaps my neighbor down the hall had seen me come home and was stopping by, but it was strange because I had just walked in and no one was out there.

There was no knock, so after a second I went about my business. I'd just opened myself a cold drink and was about to have a seat when there was a second thump from the hallway.

I was really curious at this point, so I went over and opened my door. There right in front of my door stood two boys, maybe between ten and twelve years of age.

Now, mind you, they weren't filthy or anything, but the clothing they had on looked old and outdated. It made me think perhaps they were street kids or something. They were standing there, side-by-side, and they both had their heads tilted down a bit, looking at the floor. The whole sight shouldn't have bothered me but for some reason it did. Just their presence made me uneasy.

I looked around and up and down the hall. I was hoping there were some adults around but there was no one else in sight. I turned back to take a look at those kids and they were both looking up at me. One of them says, "We're here for a visit; we want to come in and watch the telly."

I felt so very strange when this child spoke. There was something I couldn't put my finger on and it made me very uncomfortable. Thinking they were simply lost and at the wrong place, I responded.

"Sorry, I think you lot have the wrong flat."

The same boy responded in a cold tone.

"Well, we'll come in anyway. Just ask us in now."

I just stood there and both of those boys looked up a little more. It was then that I saw their faces clearly. I realized with a start that their eyes were solid black, not a single speck of white showing. I couldn't believe it; it completely unnerved me. I tried my best to act normal. I looked away, down the hall again, but then I looked back at the boys a bit closer. There were other things that just didn't seem right.

Their skin was very pale and had sort of a pasty appearance, it didn't look very natural at all, and it had a weird texture to it. The same boy spoke once again, insisting on watching some telly.

Now, I've lived in several places around the world. I did part of my schooling in the United States and I've heard a lot of accents. This boy sounded like he was doing a very bad impression of a British accent. None of it was making any sense.

I tried to take it all in, those black eyes, the pasty skin, odd clothing, and now a forced accent. Everything about the situation told me that something was wrong here, and yet, I felt myself compelled to listen to them. Some part of me just wanted to open my door to these young boys.

That boy was saying the same things, over and over again. I felt my hand on the knob, slowly opening the door a little more. All the while, I felt a panic setting in. What in the world would happen if I let these children just come in?

I turned my head about and looked inside my flat. I don't know what I was thinking, perhaps to grab a weapon or perhaps I was thinking about running inside and how quickly I could close the door. It's very difficult to explain the divided thoughts racing about in my head. When I turned and looked back at the boys, I was startled to see that there were now three of them.

They had multiplied.

The third boy looked like the other two; they could have all been brothers. There's no way I wouldn't have seen him when I was looking right at those kids. He was standing right behind the first two and staring at me just like the others. He had the same solid, black eyes as they did.

The lead boy spoke to me again, a little louder now, saying,

"Just...invite...us...in...mate."

It was cold and creepy and it gave me a chill I'll never forget. It was enough to jolt me into action. I promptly stepped back and slammed the door on those kids, and bolted it shut.

Once in my flat, I was shaking my head. I was feeling foggy and unclear as if I'd had a bit too much to drink; I wish I really had been drinking; it was all so strange. I was trying to figure out what was happening.

I dashed over to the phone to ring my neighbor down the hall to have him come out. Just as I picked up the receiver and started to dial, I heard those strange thumps outside the door again. First one, then a pause, then another.

I put the phone down and listened. After a few minutes, I went back over and cracked the door open slowly, just enough to see out. The hallway looked empty. I opened the door the rest of the way and had a look around. The hallway was completely empty; the children were gone.

I looked down the stairs and there wasn't a soul in sight. I even went to the end of the hallway and looked out the window towards the street. There was no sign of those children."

While Richard's account fits the bill of standard BEK encounters, he also reports some unusual aspects exhibited during the incident. The loud 'thumps' he reports are unique and Richard believes, based on the timing, that the noise marked both the arrival and the departure of the children. Richard reflects on the sound:

"You know, it wasn't too loud, but it was like something dropping from several feet in the air. Something with a little weight to it. I've always felt like those children sort of dropped in from somewhere. I don't know why I heard the sound when they left though. Still, it's what I've always felt."

Of course, the most startling aspect in Richard's account is the seeming ability of the children to multiply. Granted, it's possible Richard was merely distracted by the whole event and didn't notice the third child at first. Perhaps the additional boy was hiding behind the first two when the encounter started. Still, Richard felt that he only turned for a few seconds, and he firmly believes he would have seen movement with his peripheral vision. Not only that, but the hallway is small, and while a third child could have been hiding, it would have been difficult. If the extra child was hiding initially, then he had to move very quickly and very quietly to take his position with his cohorts.

During Richard's entire encounter with the children, they were very still and rigid in their stance. Only their heads moved, and even then, only when the lead child began to speak. Richard noted that their arms hung straight down at their sides and they never made any threatening gestures.

I have since received additional accounts from the UK but none of them contain these unusual aspects. As more encounters from this area of the world are reported, it will be interesting to see if there are any others like Richard's experience.

While the children who appeared at Richard's apartment attempted to adapt a British accent, some witnesses report that the children can speak other languages fluently.

Hector's Story

Hector is from Mexico, is fluent in Spanish, and speaks English well, having lived in the United States for several years. He works at his family's Mexican restaurant in San Antonio, Texas. Hector had an encounter with a black eyed child while at work one weekend.

"One of the cooks came and told me there was a boy hanging around outside at the back of the restaurant. He thought maybe the kid was digging in the trash or something. He saw him when he took a bag of trash out to the dumpster. The boy was watching him but turned his face away and went behind the dumpster when the cook looked towards him. The dumpster has a gate all around it, but we leave it open during business hours. Sometimes we get homeless people going through the trash bins. I think it's sad, but it's also a problem for us because they throw the trash all around on the ground, so we

have to keep them away.

I went out back and didn't see anyone at first. I walked over to the dumpster, looked in the gate, then walked all around the outside of it; there was no one in sight. It's just a parking area back there and it's usually empty.

I figured the kid had run off after seeing the cook so I headed back inside. Just as I closed the door behind me there was a loud knock on it. It was very strange, I don't know how someone could have run up to the door so quickly. There was nothing close to the building to hide behind.

I opened the door and there was this boy. He had a hooded sweatshirt on and he had the hood pulled pretty far forward. He looked at me and sort of pushed his face forward. His eyes were solid black. I know to this day exactly what I saw. I know I must have looked very shocked. The boy spoke to me in Spanish. He said, "I knew you would be the one to open the door. Now you're in for it."

That boy just started laughing. It was a loud laugh and it scared me. I slammed the door shut. It was just my reaction to that boy. Right away the laughing stopped. I told everyone to leave the door shut and not to go outside. Then I called the police and told them there was a homeless person out back that wouldn't leave. I didn't know what else to tell them, but I wasn't going out there myself. When the police got there, they couldn't find anybody around and the boy never returned."

Hector was convinced that somehow the boy had come out of nowhere since there was nothing he could have used to hide. He also believed the black eyed child somehow cast bad luck on him since a series of things happened right after this encounter.

"I left work that evening and I had a flat tire on the way home. The tires were new and had only been on for two weeks. I didn't run over anything; the tire just split apart. When I returned it, the mechanic said he'd never seen that happen with those tires but it must have just been faulty. That wasn't all though. That same night at home, the oven caught on fire in our kitchen, I was lucky to get it put out before it damaged our home. The strange thing was, the oven had been used early that night but had been off for probably an hour. We went to church for a midnight mass. I said a lot of prayers and lit a candle to make this go away. That was finally the end of it and I hope that black eyed boy never comes back."

Was Hector the victim of a trickster? He believes that whatever the child represented, it was responsible for the misfortunes he experienced that night. Hector believes going to mass and saying prayers for protection kept he and his family from suffering any further misfortunes cast on him by the boy.

This black eyed child had blonde hair, very white skin, and was fluent in Spanish, at least when he spoke to Hector. Of course, anyone can learn a language, but this is exactly the kind of behavior we would expect from a trickster. The chaos created in Hector's life led him to question things on a spiritual level.

"Months after I saw that boy, I was still thinking about it," he said.

"I never thought about spiritual things that much but this experience led me to start exploring and learning more about my culture's spiritual roots."

In the time following his encounter, Hector delved into the traditional healing methods and spiritual traditions passed down by his grandparents. He has continued to learn and grow on a spiritual level and wants to eventually teach and help people understand that there's more in the world than people think about during their nine-to-five lives.

"I still go to mass all the time, but I practice other spiritual traditions too. The two do not conflict in my heart. I believe that some higher force sent that black eyed boy to wake me up and send my life in a different direction. It was a brush with something that I still don't understand, but I do my best to keep moving forward and to follow what God wants me to do."

Hector's encounter with the black eyed child was brief, but it caused him to change his very path in life and to seek a deeper spiritual meaning of human existence. That is, after all, the nature of the trickster. Wherever it goes, the trickster brings chaos. The trickster is the very force of change and transformation created by turmoil and disaster. Is it possible the black eyed children are yet another manifestation of the trickster archetype?

Considering the upheaval their appearance usually creates, it's a good possibility. Not only do the BEKs create upheaval, but encounters with them often lead to personal transformation for the witness. This is the very nature of the trickster dynamic. We must also remember, change is created not just for the witness, but for those close to him. Black eyed kid encounters influence a wide and expanding circle of people.

Native elders tell stories of Coyote's wild antics to convey lessons, information and tribal knowledge. If the BEKs represent modern tricksters, what do the tales communicate? It's difficult to answer this completely at such an early stage in the modern accounts, but one thing is clear, the black eyed children are creating domino effects each time they make an appearance, and like the trickster, the chaos left in their wake is causing change.

Chapter II

The Djinn

The djinn are supernatural beings whose origins lie in the Middle East. Perhaps better known to the western world as 'genies,' these beings are mentioned in the classic collection of folktales, "One Thousand and One Nights." They are also mentioned numerous times in the Muslim holy book, the Quran, as well as other Islamic religious texts.

Arab folklore and Islamic teachings talk about the mystical djinn and the vast array of magical powers the beings possess. They are considered one of the three sentient creations of Allah, the other two being angels and humans.

The djinn exist in a world parallel to ours. Like humans, they can be either good or evil, benevolent or malicious. Islamic teachings talk about Allah's creation of the djinn. While humans were created out of clay, the djinn were made from 'smokeless flame' or 'scorching fire.' Like humans, the djinn have free will, but were expected to worship Allah and follow the teachings of the prophet.

In the early days of creation, a djinn known as Iblis abused his freedoms. In front of Allah, he refused to bow to the authority of Adam when Allah ordered both the angels and the djinn to do so. For this disobedience, Iblis and his followers were cast out of paradise and deemed 'shaytan' or in modern terms, Satan. While some evidence exists that the djinn may have been worshiped in some areas, Islamic teaching warns against this.

115

The Quran states:

"Yet they make the djinn equals with Allah, though Allah did create the djinn; and they falsely, having no knowledge, attribute to Him sons and daughters. Praise and glory be to Him! (for He is) above what they attribute to Him!" Quran 6:100

The djinn have life spans and powers that far exceed that of mortals. They can travel vast distances in the blink of an eye. They can shape-shift into any form from human to animal, even into the form of a tree, or an inanimate object. They are also able to take possession of other living beings, controlling both the mind and body of their chosen victim. The djinn are notorious for affecting the minds of humans. They can enter dreams and appear as vile creatures, or as loved ones long departed. They can whisper in people's ears, assuming the role of 'helpful' spirits and passing along secrets and prophetic information. It is rarely for beneficial reasons.

Rosemary Ellen Guiley has written an excellent study of these mysterious beings, *"The Djinn Connection: The Hidden Links Between Djinn, Shadow People, ETs, Nephilim, Archons, Reptilians and Other Entities."*

Guiley promotes the idea that the djinn may account for a large portion of encounters with various paranormal entities such as demons and extraterrestrials. While she does not discount the possibility of other supernatural beings existing, she believes the shape shifting djinn may be using the cultural concept of such things in order to interfere with humans. Are the djinn really this powerful and pervasive? It's quite possible they represent a class of beings we simply don't yet understand and that few people are ready to accept.

Their ability to shape shift may make it easier for the djinn to insert themselves into the lives of people unaware of their existence. In the United States for example, few people have heard of the djinn outside of fairy tales. Extraterrestrials, however, are a common media image. Are the djinn appearing as ETs in order to disrupt the lives of their victims? If the djinn are truly such powerful beings, we may have little idea of the true scope of their power.

Encounters with the Djinn

According to Middle Eastern beliefs, the djinn live in cities and lead regular lives, albeit, on a different level of existence than ours. They have families and relationships, and may even choose to follow a religious path.

These 'Hidden Ones,' as they are sometimes called, commonly reside in deserted places. Deserts, wastelands, graveyards, even the very air around us can be home to the djinn. Some areas gain a reputation as dwelling places of djinn and such places are usually avoided by humans as a precaution against encountering the magical beings.

A Sufi friend of mine, Nazim, is quite familiar with traditions surrounding the djinn:

"You must be careful, especially at night if you are near a graveyard or deserted place because the djinn are always near, waiting for opportunities. They will possess you if they have the chance because they like to meddle with humans and cause trouble. In America, most people think the djinn are funny cartoons, but that is far, far from the truth."

Nazim lives in the United States, but has spent a lot of time in the Middle East. He says people in the Middle East still have a lot of awareness of the djinn and their power.

"Sometimes in the desert, you will hear music, it comes from nowhere because there is nothing as far as you can see. This music is the djinn. They are invisible to us unless they want to reveal themselves. I have been in the deserts and have heard their music; it is an eerie sound. Also, they will throw stones at you sometimes. Again, there will be nothing as far as you can see, no other people.

Three of us were out together one night, it is safer in groups, but we were not safe that night. The djinn pelted us with stones, small ones about the size of a quarter at first, then larger ones. We got away as quickly as we could, saying prayers the whole time."

According to Nazim, summoning the djinn really isn't hard, as they are always waiting for opportunities to access the human world:

"The djinn are always around, and they are not confined to the Middle East despite what some people believe. Just as humans have spread around the world, so have the djinn. If you speak about them too much, they will hear you and they will come, so it is best to speak in whispers if you need to talk about them."

Nazim believes the djinn are masters at setting traps and finding an individual's weakness:

"Like a spider, a djinn will very slowly spin a web until it surrounds you. He will tell you what you wish to hear and appear as a helpful spirit. He will even tell you to pray and follow spiritual teachings. He will do whatever is necessary to draw you in until you are trapped. Once you go willingly, it is very difficult to get away. The djinn can drive you insane."

Nazim related the story of a man he met from Egypt who contracted with a djinn:

"He knew it was a djinn when it came to him, but he thought this was a good djinn. I do not think there is any such thing. No one else could see the djinn, but this man could. This man took the djinn's advice in his business and eventually even his personal life. It got to be that he could not make any choice himself until the djinn told him what to do. The djinn would tell him what suit to wear, what to eat and when to pray.

Then things got very bad. The djinn would not stop talking, whispering in the man's ear all the time, even when he tried to sleep. The djinn would send him on meaningless journeys and make him do ridiculous tasks. The man lost his wife and his business. His health began to fail very quickly.

Finally, his brother helped him find a holy man who could take care of it. The holy man said that the djinn had possessed this man and had to be cast out."

Once the deceitful djinn had been exorcised, the man was on the road to recovery. According to Nazim, it took another year for all the effects to wear off and for the man's life to return to normal.

Tradition suggests it is possible to summon djinn, but this is a dangerous proposition. These beings are very difficult to control and only a Sheikh (Islamic holy man), or a sorcerer, is likely to have the ability to bind such a being and force it to do what is asked. Ancient texts containing details of ceremonies to summon djinn are still available, and can be accessed by modern magic workers in their quest to control these powerful creatures. Despite the dangers, sorcerers are said to utilize djinn to carry out difficult tasks and even to harm people. Under the direction of a magician, a djinn may cast the evil eye, create accidents, and cause illness or even death.

The djinn can exist independently, but they can also be bound to objects such as rings or amulets. No one can forget the famous tale of Aladdin and the Wonderful Lamp with its magical genie. Some of these tales may come from legends of sorcerers attempting to control djinn by binding them to physical objects.

King Solomon enslaved the djinn and they attended him in his temple. According to the Quran, Solomon bound the magical beings and forced them to perform tasks in his temple until his death. The Quran states:

"And before Solomon were marshaled his hosts, of djinn and men and birds and they were all kept in order and ranks" Quran 27:17.

The Quran says Solomon died standing upright, leaning on his staff. The djinn, unaware the king had died, continued to perform their tasks. They did so until Allah sent a worm out of the ground to eat away at Solomon's staff, causing the king's body to collapse. The Quran states:

"Then, when we decreed (Solomon's) death, nothing showed them his death except a little worm of the earth, which kept gnawing away at his staff so when he fell down, the djinn saw plainly that if they had known the unseen, they would not have tarried in the humiliating penalty." Quran 34:14.

Some people believe that, once free from Solomon's control, the djinn became more malicious. Angry at having been trapped for so long, they forever seek to manipulate humans in their quest for revenge. Many early scholars portray the djinn as evil, demonic beings, reveling in the use of their powers over humans and continually on a quest for revenge.

In Ibn Taymeeyah's *Essay on the Jinn,* he says they were generally *"ignorant, untruthful, oppressive and treacherous."*

Furthermore, he believes the power of the djinn account for much of what passes for magic. Mimicking the voices of the departed during seances, revealing hidden secrets to fortunetellers, and assisting magicians, are all djinn tricks designed to deceive humans. While a few traditions claim the djinn will grant wishes and offer assistance to humans, most accounts point to them being masters of deception and lies. There may be good djinn, but considering their skills, bargaining with them hardly seems to be worth the risk.

The djinn may be relatively unknown dwellers in the world of the paranormal, but if they are as widespread and powerful as some research suggests, exploring their existence may change the face of our already strange world.

The number of correlations between djinn and the black eyed children certainly warrants further attention. As master shape shifters, it would be no problem for the djinn to take the guise of a BEK. Likewise, the chaos created in the lives of those who meet the children matches the pattern of the djinn's desire to create trouble for humans. Curses and ill fortune? Right up the djinn's alley. The ability to appear or vanish suddenly? Again, well within the province of the djinn. If the djinn are by chance behind the rash of black eyed children encounters, the problem of the BEKs may be much more significant, and much more dangerous, than it first appears.

Chapter 12

Dark Thoughts

A thoughtform is a creation of pure mental energy. Some ancient traditions teach that the mind can be directed and focused to manifest on the physical level. Essentially, this means that with enough mental focus, a 'thought' or image can become physically tangible. Could this explain some or all of the black eyed children accounts?

What if the BEKs are not physical beings in the way we understand the concept? Is it possible they are beings conjured by the human mind?

Thoughtforms and Tulpas

The belief in thoughtforms is ancient and was especially prominent in the Far East. The concept was developed extensively by Buddhist monks in Tibet. Tibetan mysticism teaches that a thoughtform can be created by a specific series of meditations that focus the energy of the mind toward manifestation. Tibetans refer to a being created this way as a 'tulpa.'

A tulpa starts as a simple image in the mind. Over time, it gains a greater degree of physical existence, moving from an image in the mind's eye, to a phantom or spectral image, and finally, to full physical manifestation. A living, physical being created by the power of the human mind. Once in solid form, a tulpa can continue to exist in the physical world, provided it receives the energy it needs. This is usually provided by people continuing to believe in its existence, hence, 'feeding' the tulpa mental energy.

Thoughtforms gained a lot of attention in the early 1900's among Theosophists. Theosophists followed an esoteric tradition that blended various religious and occult practices into what they believed was a greater overall system. When esoteric knowledge from the far east began to make its way to the west, Theosophists and followers of other western magical traditions began to mix Tibetan spiritual concepts into their practices. Two prominent Theosophists, Annie Besant and C.W. Leadbeater wrote a bestselling book entitled *"Thought Forms."* According to Besant and Leadbeater, thoughtforms can be divided into three classes:

"That which takes the image of the thinker."

"That which takes the image of some material object."

"That which takes a form entirely its own, expressing its inherent qualities in the matter which it draws round it."

It is this third classification that concerns us in cases of the black eyed children. This form of tulpa, or thoughtform, represents a free-floating energy, looking for a guise to adopt. If we are to accept the possibility of rogue energy searching for an expression of its inherent qualities, then manifestation as a black eyed child could be the chosen vessel.

If these beings are attempting to catch their victims unaware in order to provoke intense reactions, the form of the black eyed kids fits the bill. A sinister being in the form of a child is both disturbing and disarming but what would such an uncontrolled energy in physical form do? What would its purpose be?

In his book, *"The Real Men In Black,"* author Nick Redfern makes an argument for the Men In Black, or, MIB, being manifestations of tulpas. What's interesting is, his argument could well apply to the black eyed children. Redfern states:

"The Tulpa thrive on high states of emotion. In the case of the Men In Black, that high state of emotion would be pure fear. This, one could argue, would perhaps explain why the MIB are always careful to ensure they instill terror in witnesses of UFO activity—even when the case itself may not be of any high degree of significance or importance."

If we substitute the BEKs for the Men in Black in this description, it seems to fit the mold perfectly. The black eyed children show up, seemingly at random, and instill fear in those they encounter. They do not force their way inside; indeed, it would seem the act of shocking their victim is the whole point of the encounter. Perhaps the true goal is not to 'come inside' at all. It may all be a ruse to generate fear, anxiety, and high states of emotion. After all, if the BEKs were truly trying to trick people, why not hide their strange eyes or disguise themselves by other means?

Redfern continues:

"In other words, it is the fear-drenched response of the witness — rather than the actual intricacies of the UFO encounter itself—that is of vital importance to the Men In Black. It is this, more than anything else, that dictates their actions and sustains their existence in our world."

Once again, this could well explain the true purpose of the strange kids with black eyes. If they need high states of emotion in order to 'feed,' then they have developed a process to achieve just that. Thoughtforms require energy to maintain their continued existence. If that required energy can be achieved by feeding on the emotions of others, it would explain some of the bizarre BEK encounters. Fear is a powerful emotion, and if the black eyed children have discovered some way to trigger it suddenly, then they have a virtual buffet awaiting them on any given night.

Ella's account

Ella confronted a pair of black eyed children and has come to believe they were a manifestation of negative energy that somehow coalesced into the physical form of the children she encountered.

"I don't believe they were physical kids. I mean, when it happened, I think they were as solid as anything else, but the way they vanished, I don't think they were physical, living beings like we are."

Ella encountered the children while she was walking home one evening. She rounded a corner onto the street leading to her apartment and was confronted by two boys. They wore what she called 'ratty clothes' and appeared to be in their early teens.

"They were just there and the weird thing is that no one else was around

anywhere. I looked up and down the street and no one else was out. Those boys, only one of them talked, they wanted me to take them to my apartment. It was pretty creepy."

The children insisted Ella take them to her place, but they didn't threaten her specifically.

"I can't tell you why I felt threatened, I just did. They kept their hands hanging down beside them and they weren't holding a weapon or anything, it was just a menacing way that the boy insisted that I had to invite them over. I pulled my cell phone out of my purse and looked down to dial it. I was calling a friend, but I thought maybe if they believed I was calling the police they'd leave me alone. When I looked back up, they were gone—that quickly. There was nowhere for them to go, no alley, nothing to hide behind. I looked all around. They would have had to run a long way before they could have been out of my field of vision. I couldn't get home fast enough. I locked the doors and tried to forget about it."

Ella recounts that when she saw the black eyed children, she was experiencing an especially bad stage in her life. A series of difficult relationships, job changes, family issues, and health concerns had taken a toll on her mentally and emotionally. On reflection, after her encounter, she began believing the BEKs were somehow a manifestation of the negativity within and around her.

"The more I thought about those kids, the more I started thinking they were some kind of hallucination. I was at a really bad point in my life, a lot of negative things had happened. In some weird way, those two black eyed boys represented all the bad things going on with me. It was like all the negative energy around me in physical form and they scared the hell out of me. Even on the day of the encounter, I was walking around all day wondering if something worse was going to happen to me. I admit it sounds silly, but it was as if my bad thoughts somehow took form and confronted me."

Trials, ordeals, and life changes are some of the common, connecting factors among BEK witnesses. Reactions to the experiences range from pursuit of a more spiritual lifestyle to trauma-like symptoms. Confronting negative energy in the form of a child is difficult for the adult mind to process. This may be the very reason the subconscious mind uses such a form. It is unsettling, disturbing, and requires a great deal of time to come to terms with. A person continually haunted by their encounter with the black eyed children will continue to 'feed' the thoughtform, thus giving the black eyed beings exactly what they wanted. It is the continued feeding of emotional energy, and the ongoing belief in a thoughtform, that allows it to continue to exist. Belief in this level of manifestation is not limited to eastern traditions.

Mexican shaman Don Juan Matus spoke about the true nature of the physical universe and the ability to manifest. Working with his student, author Carlos Castaneda, Don Juan taught Castaneda that intense levels of concentration can materialize objects from thin air. Castaneda himself was said to have materialized a squirrel on Don Juan's hand by following his teacher's instructions.

Why would a thoughtform, or tulpa, take the form of a child with black eyes? This may be the result of the subconscious mind of the person encountering the children. If the deeper recesses of the mind are desperate to facilitate a change in one's life, then anything is possible. For most people, a child represents innocence. Black eyes, on the other hand, are equated with something sinister or outright evil. The two symbols clash and the very fact that they clash may work as shock therapy for the mind.

BEKs and the Shadow Self

Swiss psychiatrist Carl Jung wrote:

"Everyone carries a shadow, and the less it is embodied in the individual's conscious life, the blacker and denser it is."

Jung believed this shadow aspect could appear in dreams, visions, and other forms. According to Jung, the shadow often appears with 'dark features.' Perhaps the black eyed children are a physical manifestation of this hidden, shadow aspect.

Jungian psychology teaches that the shadow is a part of the unconscious mind made up of repressed shortcomings and weaknesses. The shadow is created in the mind of the individual and is very personal. However, cultural and societal influence also have a bearing on the shadow's nature. The shadow can play many different roles in one's life. Interacting with shadow aspects can offer insight into one's state of mind. The shadow is often confrontational, signifying qualities that either are in opposition to, or suppressed by, the individual. Jung said:

"The shadow personifies everything that the subject refuses to acknowledge about himself."

According to Jung, the primal and irrational nature of the shadow make it prone to projection. If left unchecked, this instinctive projection can cripple the individual and lead to illusion.

"The projection-making factor then has a free hand and can realize its object—if it has one—or bring about some other situation characteristic of its power."

Jung believed dealing with the shadow played a central part in the process of becoming an individual. Through confronting the shadow self, he said, the individual would have the opportunity to confront, and hopefully, overcome negative aspects of the self. Despite its negative nature, Jung believed the shadow was the seat of creativity. For those willing to confront the shadow and integrate it, a greater level of consciousness and a stronger sense of self is possible.

Jungians believe confrontation with the shadow is a continuing process however, and great care must be taken so the individual is not overwhelmed by his own shadow self.

If the BEKs are not a manifestation of the individual shadow, they may come from the collective unconscious of humanity. Carl Jung coined the term collective unconscious to describe a part of the unconscious mind expressed in humans. While the personal unconscious is created within an individual, the collective unconscious is inherited. This represents a universal set of archetypes and forms that are pre-existent within each of us. While the individual's unconsciousness is a personal storehouse of experience, the collective unconscious links each member of a species.

The concept branches off into the idea of a 'world mind' and Jung himself even hinted at such a possibility. The concept is not as hard to believe as one might think. Studies have shown that multiple people focusing on a specific goal can achieve some incredible things.

The Power of Many Minds

One of the most remarkable, documented examples of group focus occurred in Washington D.C. in the early 1990's, when a transcendental meditation experiment caused a dramatic drop in violent crime.

The project involved four thousand practitioners of the

transcendental meditation technique. Participants gathered from around the world and stayed in hotels and college dormitories throughout the D.C. metro area. The designated period for the experiment was June 7th through July 30th. Participants practiced group meditation around the clock during this period. Violent crime, which included murders, rapes, and assaults,dropped by an amazing 23 percent.

Lest anyone think the organization was trying to mislead people, the experiment was given a rigorous analysis by a review board of independent civic leaders and scientists. Psychologist David Orme-Johnson was not surprised at the effects of the meditation experiment:

"The conventional scientific model has assumed that individual consciousness is completely separate from that of others, and that there is no common field linking us together. But the most subtle energy fields are at the basis of everything in the universe. Why then shouldn't we expect that human consciousness also has field characteristics at more fundamental levels?"

Similar experiments have been conducted in other violent locations around the world. Results from these experiments are important because they demonstrate the impact of focused meditation and the effects it can create.

Dr. David Edwards from the University of Texas at Austin noted:

"This work and the theory that informs it deserve the most serious consideration by academics and policymakers alike."

Clearly, such studies indicate it is possible to influence the group consciousness with proper focus. Considering these possibilities, and Jung's concept regarding projections of the collective unconscious, it may be that paranormal entities owe a good deal of their existence to the group mind.

Such an explanation would account for things like sudden appearances and disappearances, and the fact that only certain people seem to encounter weird entities. Perhaps they are simply more 'open' to the influence of the group mind and its projections.

Considering the dire situation much of the world is now facing, the black eyed children may be a manifestation of deeply repressed fear and anger. This means there may be a deeper message inherent in sightings of the black eyed kids. While it's doubtful anyone 'wants' to see the black eyed children, the subconscious mind may have other ideas. Much like a mirage in the desert, the kids may be showing up because of some stress or inner desire to have a change in their life situation.

If not inner stress, then the beings could be projections of the collective mind attempting to convey information about mass consciousness.

People are becoming more aware, opening spiritually, and seeking answers to the mysteries of the world around us. As things shift on a global scale, so do our perceptions. The last few years have seen dramatic increases in reported encounters with the paranormal. Are we growing more aware, or are supernatural entities becoming more active?

Likewise, we must consider the effect planetary strife is having on the collective unconscious. Are the black eyed children a manifestation of the world's shadow self? A deep message from the collective unconscious about the human condition? From here on out, anything's possible.

Chapter 13

Haunted Dreams

One of the most common aftereffects reported by those who encounter the black eyed children is a disruption of sleeping habits, and unusual or troubling dreams. Witnesses report sleepless nights, strange dreams, and at times, nightmares. Some people find they are only able to sleep during daylight hours after their experience with the children. For most, the effects are temporary or sporadic. Witnesses report varying degrees of issues with sleep lasting anywhere from a few weeks to several months after a BEK encounter.

Dale encountered a trio of black eyed children in Dallas, Texas. For weeks, he was haunted by them in his dreams and thought they had returned:

"For weeks on end, after I saw the kids, I would wake up in the middle of the night. It would always be sudden. I would bolt up in bed from a dead sleep. I would sit up, thinking that something was tapping on my bedroom window. I always had to calm myself down before taking a look over at the window. I'd get up and look outside, but there wouldn't be anything there.

It was like those dreams when you're falling and you feel like you hit the bed and it wakes you up. It's shocking and you're not sure if you really hit the bed or if it was the dream.

The knocks were the same. I'd hear it as though it was in the dream but really happening in my house too. Sometimes the knocks sounded like they were at the front door; other times I thought they were on my bedroom door.

I live alone, so that was even more disturbing."

Hypnotic Effects

Perhaps the dreams and nightmares are not caused by the children at all. It may be a side effect of the hypnotic techniques attempted by the BEKs.

In clinical studies, strange dreams have been shown to be a side effect of hypnosis. If the black eyed children are attempting to use some type of programming, hypnotic suggestion or mind control, there could very well be side effects as a result. Many encounters with the children result in the witness feeling as if hypnosis had been attempted on them.

Karla, who encountered the children in Minneapolis, Minnesota, recalled the feeling the BEK produced:

"I've been hypnotized before by a professional hypnotist. I used it to quit smoking a couple of years ago. I had a whole series of sessions so I got familiar with the feeling of being put under.

When this kid started talking to me, it gave me the same feeling. He was saying things like, 'invite me in' and 'offer me a drink of water.' It was a little startling to remember later what that familiar feeling was and where I had experienced it before."

Karla says she does not believe the kids were successful in planting hypnotic suggestions in her mind:

"The hypnotist who I saw had to work with me in the first couple of sessions just to get me to relax and allow myself to go into a hypnotic state. He said that my mind was resistant to it and I'd have to get past that barrier in order to let him help me. I finally felt a difference and really relaxed by the third appointment with him. I did have great results and believe that the hypnosis sessions helped me stop smoking.

Of course, I'm not about to let just anybody hypnotize me you know, especially not some strange kid standing on my doorstep. If that's what they were trying, and it felt like it to me, then they picked the wrong person."

The failed attempt at hypnosis on Karla didn't result in any issues for her in the aftermath of her encounter. She reports she suffered no nightmares and no change in her sleep patterns.

Others aren't so lucky. Jenny, a witness in Arizona, had numerous personal issues after her meeting with the children. She sent me her account of an experience she had while working at a gas station/convenience mart outside of Phoenix. Her encounter occurred in 2009 while she was working a late-night shift.

Jenny's Story

"I was working the closing shift like always. My boyfriend worked late and we only had one car so it worked out better that way. By the time I finished my closing duties, he could come and pick me up. This happened one night after the store had been closed for about fifteen minutes. Since we have pay at the pump gas, the lights stay on all night and the whole area's very well lit. There's always lots of people coming and going. I never worried about any trouble because the only problem we'd ever had were a couple of drunks now and then. It wasn't an area where you had to worry about crime or violence at the time. I was in the back room behind the registers doing my paperwork when there was a knock on the front glass doors. It happens sometimes, people still think I can let them in for a soda or something. Usually they'll get the hint in a couple of minutes and go away but this time the knock wouldn't stop. It was also weird because it was a constant rapping, a long drawn out knock, knock, knock. I thought the person must be really determined or maybe it was another drunk. As a safety precaution, store policy was to never open the doors after hours. Usually, it was best to just stay in the back room and let the person at the door think that everyone had gone home.

That knocking though, it just wouldn't stop and I couldn't drown it out. I can usually ignore things like that, but for some reason, it made it so I couldn't even concentrate. I'd start counting the drawer and then forget what I had counted. This happened maybe twice and the third time I got up. I tried to look out through the crack of the door but I couldn't see who it was out front. I decided to turn some of the inside lights off, hoping that would make the person go away. That knocking kept on though. Finally, I got up and headed for the door, planning to yell at the person that we were closed and tell them to just leave.

When I got around the counter, I saw two kids standing at the glass doors. My first thought was that their parents must be out pumping gas but when I looked in the lot, there weren't any cars and there was no one else in sight. What in the world were two kids doing out at this time of night?

135

In a loud voice, I asked, "Where are your parents?" The kids just stood there looking at me but they didn't answer. They were standing about an arm's length from the doors and I thought this whole thing was a little strange. There were two of them and their clothes looked a bit worn. They were wearing those hoodies that kids wear but I thought that something looked unusual about their clothes. It's like the clothes didn't quite fit them right. I know that baggy clothes are popular with some kids, but it wasn't just that, something looked wrong. I asked them again where their parents were but they didn't answer; they just stared at me. I started to wonder if they were a couple of homeless kids.

I know I shouldn't have done it but being a mother, I couldn't help myself. I opened that door thinking the kids were in some kind of trouble and maybe needed help. I turned the lock and opened the door enough to get my head out and asked the kids if they were okay.

"Are you kids lost? Do you need help? Can I call someone to pick you up?"

The kids just stood there for a moment then one of them said, "We want to come in and shop."

As soon as that boy spoke, I got a really bad feeling in my stomach. All of a sudden, I was afraid of what was going on. Maybe this was some kind of gang thing. I looked around the lot again, hoping to see some other people but nobody was there. I looked back at the kids and it seemed like they were closer to me now. It was the weirdest thing because I should have seen them move even with my head turned some.

I wanted to close that door so bad but for some odd reason I was having a hard time making myself do it. It seemed like I stood there thinking about closing the door, trying to push it shut and lock it but at the same time part of me was refusing my brain's order to close the door. I felt stuck.

I told the kids that we were closed and I asked again where their parents were.

They just ignored my question and the same boy spoke again telling me, "Invite us in to shop.... we know you can."

Each time he said the word 'shop' it had a hard sound. It was like a kid who just learned a new word and wanted to keep practicing it.

He repeated the same thing again. Right then I looked at that boy; he was only a few feet away from me. I realized that his eyes were completely dark, there was no white in them; every bit of those eyes was black. His eyes *were so black in fact that they shined from the lights.*

I didn't hesitate anymore. I closed the door as quick as I could and ran back to get my phone. I got my boyfriend on the phone and told him to get over as quick as he could 'cause there were two creepy boys hanging around outside the store. He was already on his way so he said it would only be a few minutes. He told me to call the police if I was worried but he'd only be a couple of minutes.

Just as I hung up the phone, I heard that damn knocking on the glass start again. I don't know why I was so shaken up but I felt terrified.

I went to the back and turned on all the additional lights in the store. Then I turned the music up loud, trying to drown out the sound of that boy knocking at the door. After a few minutes, I glanced over at the doors. Those two boys were standing there, side-by-side, staring into the store. Even though I was standing behind some shelves, I felt like they were starting directly at me and they knew where I was.

I went back into the back room and called my boyfriend again, keeping him on the phone until he was pulling into the parking lot. I asked him about the creepy kids but he didn't see anyone around at all. He got out of his truck and walked around the parking lot but there was no sign of those kids.

I've never been so shaken up in my life. I didn't even finish counting money and doing paperwork that night. I put everything in the safe and decided to just go in early the next morning and take care of it all. I told my store manager about the incident and he thought they were gang members trying to rob the store. I don't think that's what they wanted though. If it was, they would have forced their way in. They didn't look or act like gang members. I asked to be taken off the night shift and I've only worked during the day after that.

I don't know what those kids were or where they came from but they scared the hell out of me."

Aftermath

Jenny's encounter with the black eyed children had lingering effects. She became ill right after the incident and was plagued by strange dreams and restless nights.

"The manager was nice; he gave me some time off so I could settle down

and try to forget the whole thing. I couldn't get past it very well though. For weeks afterwards, my nerves were a mess. I'd jump if someone came over to our house and knocked on the door. I had stomach issues for over a month and had a hard time keeping food down. I lived on crackers and water I think. Anything else that I tried to eat tasted sour to me. If someone was cooking in the house, I couldn't stand the smell of it. It wasn't only the food; I constantly thought there was something rotting around the house but no one else could smell it. I even made my boyfriend crawl around under the house because I thought that some animal had gotten under there and died, but he couldn't find anything.

Not only that, I think the worst thing was the dreams. I would dream about those kids. For a while, it was every night in a row. So much so that for a time I would try to keep myself up, watching television until I fell asleep on the sofa.

In the dreams, those kids would show up at my house, knocking on the door and telling me I had to let them in. Sometimes I would dream they were staring in the windows at me. I'd be standing at the kitchen sink and I'd look up and see them staring in the window in front of me with those creepy black eyes. I called them nightmares, but really that's the only thing that would happen in the dreams, they wouldn't hurt me or anything, but it was so frightening just seeing them show up like that staring at me with those cold eyes. I guess it would seem silly to people hearing the story but there's something very disturbing about those kids."

Jenny's story is a prime example of someone experiencing lasting effects after encountering the BEKs. Haunted by the experience long after the original incident, Jenny believes the black eyed boys somehow 'cursed' her.

In Jenny's case, the dreams became stronger as time passed. In some of the nightmares, the boys would be rapping on her windows, calling out for her to let them in. She reported that over time, the dreams tapered off to once a week or so, and, eventually got to a point where they only occurred periodically. Jenny says that when the dreams do come, there is still little variation. The black eyed boys do not harm or chase her, but they do continue to insist that she let them in.

"I just don't know what they did, but it has stuck with me for far, far too long."

Jenny continues to feel a sense of dread from the nightmares. She quit working at the convenience store not long after the incident, unable to work at the location where her encounter had occurred. She got a job working at home and became more and more reclusive. She says she still feels a nervous rush whenever there is a knock at her door.

A number of people report similar issues after encounters with the BEKs. The image of black, staring eyes locks itself into the conscious mind, and in turn, is carried into the dream state. Some people who experienced encounters years previously, report that they still, on occasion, have dreams related to the kids. As in Jenny's experience, the dreams are usually repetitive and unnerving. Even in the dream state, the black eyed children are trying to get in.

Chapter 14

When The Darkness Arrives

While working on this book I did a number of radio interviews on the topic of the black eyed children. The response was always exceptional and for weeks after each interview, I would continue to receive emails from listeners interested in the subject. Most of the communications from listeners were comments and opinions as to the nature of the BEKs. While many of the emails related 'friend of a friend' experiences, a portion were always from people who had encountered the black eyed children directly.

Many listeners were unnerved by the fact that this was a growing phenomenon and that other people had encountered the kids. Most people who have seen the children felt, and maybe hoped, they had experienced an isolated incident. They weren't inclined to discuss the matter, thinking no one would believe them, or understand what they were talking about.

Among the flood of emails were many fascinating stories, and one report that was absolutely stunning.

A woman in the Midwest had a close friend who had encountered the black eyed kids. I usually don't spend much time with these accounts because the original person is often difficult or impossible to find. This woman told me I simply had to speak to her friend, however, because the case involved a BEK who was invited in.

The incident revolved around a woman named Sharon who

lived in Iowa. A series of emails was followed by numerous phone conversations. Finally, Sharon decided to tell me the full story of her family's encounter with a black eyed child.

This is the first case I have documented wherein a BEK was actually invited in. The results were very disturbing to say the least.

Sharon's Story

Sharon is a registered nurse in a rural area of Iowa. She lives in a small town with her husband and ten-year-old son. Both Sharon's family, and her husband's family live in the same area.

Sharon's encounter with a black eyed child affected her family deeply. When she contacted me, it had been about a year and a half since the event had occurred.

It was a Sunday afternoon and Sharon had worked a long shift at the hospital. Her son had spent the night with his grandmother, so on her way home, Sharon stopped and picked him up. Sharon lived about ten miles from her mother in law. Halfway between was a convenience store where she often stopped. On this particular day, Sharon stopped at the market and ran in for a carton of milk and some cereal. She parked in front of the store and jumped out. She closed the door and left her son in the back seat of the SUV. It was a safe town; she knew the area, and she would only be a moment. She hit the automatic lock and entered the market.

Moments later, when Sharon returned to her car, she jumped in and put the bag on the passenger seat. She put the key in the ignition and turned the engine over looking up in the rearview mirror at the same time. What she saw stunned her. Staring at her in the rearview mirror was a young boy with solid black eyes.

She felt terrified. She wanted to scream, but when she opened her mouth, nothing came out. The child was staring at her with a cold glare, and he was sitting right next to her son. Unusually close in the large back seat. Seeing her son beside this boy was enough to jar her mind into action. She tried to control her panic as she jumped back out of the vehicle. She jerked open the back door and yanked her son out quickly. The boy with the black eyes simply glared at her as she pulled her son out of the vehicle. She rushed back into the convenience store, pulling her son along.

The clerk, seeing the panicked look on Sharon's face, quickly came from behind the counter and asked her what was wrong and if someone was hurt.

The only response Sharon could manage was a stammered reply.

"Someone's in my car!"

The clerk knew Sharon from her frequent visits. He rushed to the front door to see what was happening outside. He turned and asked Sharon if the intruder was armed. She shook her head no. The clerk assumed someone was trying to steal Sharon's car and expected to see the vehicle pulling away or already long gone. Going out to the parking lot, however, he found the SUV parked in front of the store. The engine was running and both the driver's door and the driver's side passenger door were standing open. The clerk approached the car carefully and looked inside. There was no sign of anyone in or around Sharon's car. The clerk scanned the rest of the parking lot, but it too was empty. He reached into the car, turned the engine off and took the keys as a precaution. He closed both doors of the car, looking around the lot again. The market was positioned in a very open area. There were no trees or other buildings close by to provide a hiding place for potential criminals. Cautiously, the clerk looked around both sides of the building, then the back. There was no sign of anyone on the premises. Perhaps the carjacker had driven off with an accomplice.

Going back inside, he assured Sharon there was no sign of anyone in her vehicle or in the entire parking lot for that matter. He asked Sharon if she had gotten a good look at the person. Was he by himself or was someone waiting for him? Was there another car he could have driven off in?

The clerk continued to ask Sharon questions but she was still too shaken to respond. She stood near the counter with her arms around her son. Not getting a response from the woman, the clerk turned toward the counter stating he was calling the police. Sharon stopped him.

"No. Don't call the police."

The clerk gave her a puzzled look. *"Why shouldn't I call the cops? Someone just tried to steal your car."*

The last thing Sharon wanted to do was to try to explain what she had seen to a police officer. They would think she was lying or delusional, and in a small town word would get around. It would cause a lot of talk and trouble she didn't want to deal with.

Sharon explained briefly to the clerk that she simply hadn't gotten a good look at the person and there was nothing she could tell the police to aid in catching him. She added that there may have been another car and the person was probably long gone.

The clerk was not happy with her response. He added that he was still going to call the police and she could tell them whatever she did remember. He didn't want any potential criminals hanging around his place of business. He often worked late and there were other customers to consider.

"Look," she said, *"I don't want to make a big deal out of this because it was just a kid. Maybe he was just playing around or something but I don't think we need the police out chasing some kid that I can't even describe. Why don't you just keep an eye out and if some suspicious kid comes back around, call the police then."*

The clerk, while hesitant, gave up at this point and finally agreed with Sharon. *"I suppose if it was just a kid we can forget about it."* He asked if there was anything he could do for her and she replied no, she just wanted to go home.

Still shaken, Sharon decided to call her husband. She wanted to get her son home but she just couldn't bring herself to drive her SUV. She couldn't shake the image of the boy staring at her in the rearview mirror. Sharon pulled out her cell phone and quickly called her husband, worried that the clerk would still want to report the incident to the police. She reached her husband, Tom, with just a couple of rings and asked him to come and meet her at the store right away.

Not only was Tom puzzled at his wife's request, he had never heard such a strange tone from her before. He reached the store in a few minutes and his wife and son came outside to meet him. Sharon explained briefly to her husband that someone had "gotten into" her SUV while it was parked in front of the store. Her husband quickly asked if she and their son were okay.

"I'm just really shaken," she replied. *"The clerk came out and checked and couldn't find anyone but I just don't want to drive the SUV."*

"It was only a kid," she tried to reassure her husband. *"It just startled me and I'm feeling strange. Can you drive my SUV back and we'll*

take your truck home?"

Sharon wasn't ready to explain the details to her husband. She wanted to get home, calm down, and then talk to him about what she had seen. He agreed to her request, put the two of them in his truck and watched them pull out of the parking lot.

Tom decided to go in and talk to the clerk for a moment. He knew the man and wanted to find out if he had seen anything or could give him more information. His wife was upset and may have missed something. The clerk assured Tom that he had checked the parking lot himself and that he had walked all around the store but could find no sign of an intruder. He seemed a little skeptical in talking about the incident and Tom thought perhaps the clerk didn't believe his wife's story.

"Still think we should have called the police and let them handle this," the clerk grumbled.

Tom assured the man he would talk to his wife, and if he deemed it necessary, he would report it to the police himself. He went back outside and looked around the lot before getting into Sharon's SUV. Tom glanced into the back seat but there was nothing there.

He closed the door and turned over the engine. It was then he noticed a strange odor. It hit him in waves and seemed to get worse with each moment. To Tom, it smelled like dirty diapers, but it had been a long time since his son was in diapers. He looked around the SUV again to see if something was rotting in the back or under one of the seats. Finding nothing, he rolled down the windows and started for home, hoping the car would air out on the drive.

A few miles down the highway, Tom was in an accident.

The SUV ended up wrapped around a pole and was totaled. Another motorist passing by a few moments later saw the wrecked vehicle and phoned for help. Tom was rushed to the hospital. Fortunately, he escaped without any life-threatening injuries but it was feared he had a concussion.

Meanwhile, Sharon had made it home where she made a cup of tea and proceeded to speak to her son about the strange boy who was in her car.

"Where did that boy come from?" she asked her son.

"He came to the car when you were in the store," he replied.

"Do you know him from school?"

"No mommy, I just met him today."

Sharon was calmer, trying to logically examine the experience she had just had. She questioned herself, wondering why she had felt such fear from a little boy. The eyes, of course, had startled her and there were rare medical conditions that could do strange things to the eyes. Perhaps she had overreacted. There was something else though, something menacing about the boy. She couldn't shake the image of him staring at her in the mirror, or the glare he had when she pulled her son from the car.

"What did he want?" she asked.

"Oh, he said he wanted to ride to our house,I thought we could play."

"So, he just got in the car?"

"Oh no mommy, I asked him to get in. He said he wasn't allowed in unless I asked him."

Sharon felt a cold chill run up her spine at her son's comments. She couldn't imagine having that strange boy in her home.

"What's wrong mommy? Did I do something wrong?"

Before Sharon could answer, the phone rang. She was informed her husband had been in an accident and was at the hospital. She was assured his injuries were not life threatening but she quickly gathered her things, and her son, and rushed to the hospital to be with him.

The hospital kept Tom overnight for observation to ensure he didn't have any serious head trauma. He had struck his head during the accident, and as a result, was complaining of a headache. By later that evening it was gone and he seemed fine. Tom couldn't remember the accident itself. Although he tried to recall details, the last thing he could remember clearly was pulling out of the gas station parking lot and heading for home. He recalled that the foul smell lingered in the SUV even with the windows rolled down. Somewhere, along those few miles between the store and their home, something caused Tom to wreck the vehicle. The doctors believed he may have blacked out, or perhaps striking his head had caused him to forget what had caused the wreck. He told Sharon about the foul odor in the vehicle, asking if she had let something spoil or if she had left trash under the seats. Sharon told her husband that the SUV was fine when she left work and there was no odor. Tom speculated that the odor may have caused his blackout.

"It doesn't make any sense though," he told his wife. *"Even if it was some kind of gas, I had the windows down, so there should have been enough air flow to keep me awake."*

Late into the night, Sharon finally told her husband the full story of her encounter with the black eyed child in the back seat of her SUV. Tom listened intently, asking questions only after she had finished the story.

"You're sure you've never seen this boy before?"

"No, never. There was something cold about him Tom. He scared me."

She related the conversation she'd had with their son after the incident.

"What do you think it was?" she asked.

Tom had grown up in a religious environment and was more devoted to spiritual ideas than Sharon was. Without hesitation, he replied. *"I think it was something evil."*

One would hope that Sharon and Tom's story ended there, but there's more.

Tom was released from the hospital the following day, but, in the days that followed, their son became ill. At first, it appeared he had come down with a bad cold. Cold medicines did nothing to alleviate the symptoms, and his condition grew worse. The family doctor examined the child and said the boy had come down with a flu virus. He prescribed medications and sent the family on their way. A few days into the regimen, the boy developed what appeared to be measles. The doctor was puzzled. He could not verify measles and it seemed as though the child no longer had the same flu symptoms.

Over the next several weeks, the boy exhibited a wide variety of symptoms from high fevers to stomachaches, sores on the body, and blurred vision. Except for the occasional cold, their son had always been a healthy child. Constant tests by doctors could not solve the puzzle of the boy's condition. There was no evidence of disease found in his body, and there was no history of family illness that would account for the affliction. No one could determine what was causing the little boy to suffer.

Sharon and Tom were convinced their son was sick as a result of his encounter with the black eyed child. They began to pray on a regular basis and asked their family to also pray for the boy's recovery. Weeks after the first signs of being sick, the boy suddenly recovered. Sharon recalls the sudden change:

"I'll never forget it. He had been up most of the night, complaining of stomach pains, and unable to sleep. Sometime after three AM, he finally fell asleep. I dozed off in the chair next to his bed. I woke up just after sunrise and there he was, sitting up in bed."

To Sharon's surprise, her son was smiling and asking for food. She jumped up and checked his forehead. His temperature felt normal. Gone too, were the marks that resembled measles on his arms and legs.

"I started crying. I was so happy,I didn't know if it was the prayer or just a matter of time, but what mattered was that my son was okay."

The boy has remained healthy to this day. Sharon and Tom are convinced the encounter with the black eyed boy was a brush with something that doesn't belong here.

"I know that somehow that creepy boy caused my husband's accident and my son's illness. I just pray that we never see him or anything like him again."

It was only after much deliberation that Sharon and Tom decided to share their story with me and allow its inclusion in this book. They firmly believe the black eyed children are evil and are omens of ill fortune. Their hope is that through hearing about their family's experience, others will be able to avoid getting too close to these beings and suffering ill results.

"I hope that anyone who sees one of these...things...will stay far away from it. I don't know what they are but they carry something dreadful and they bring bad things to families."

Sharon's encounter contains some very disturbing elements. While I was not able to interview Tom and Sharon's son directly, their conversations with him regarding the black eyed child are very interesting.

It's evident from this account that a BEK can obtain permission to "come in" even from a child. In this case, the young boy invited the black eyed being to get in the car, not thinking anything was amiss. After all, in his eyes, this was just another child, and a potential playmate, so why would there be an issue?

Sharon did have another conversation with her son about the strange boy. She first asked if there was anything unusual about the boy, to which her son replied, *"No, he was just another kid."* Upon further questioning, Sharon directly asked her son about the boy's eyes.

"Do you remember what his eyes looked like?"

"No, there wasn't nothing special about them," he told her.

Clearly, the young man was not put off by any 'sinister' aura emitted by the black eyed kid. While most adults end up in a state of fear from their encounters, this young boy treated the incident as another normal part of his day. Sharon's son did reveal that the black eyed boy asked for an invitation into the vehicle.

"He said he wasn't allowed in unless I asked him."

This follows the pattern of typical BEK encounters. It seems that under any conditions, these beings need to receive an invitation to come in before they can do so. To Sharon's son, the boy was probably just following the rules of his parents by not accepting something without an invitation.

Sharon and Tom's son had little to say concerning the boy's appearance. His response, or lack of, to questions about the boy raises some interesting points. Did their son simply not notice the dark condition of the child's eyes, or did they simply appear completely normal to him? Is it possible children perceive the black eyed kids differently than adults do?

We have little to compare this case to. This is the first encounter I have documented wherein a BEK approached another child and engaged in an exchange. In all·other encounters, the BEKs only seem to approach adults, or, on occasion, teenagers, but never a solitary child.

We are left to wonder if there was something special about this situation that caused the BEK to approach a child. Perhaps this is a new tactic and he believed he would be able to get into Tom and Sharon's house.

And what about the strange illness the young man suffered after his encounter with the black eyed kid? Did the BEK in fact somehow 'infect' Sharon's son with some exotic disease that caused the boy to exhibit so many strange symptoms for weeks?

While Tom is convinced the boy was a manifestation of a biblical evil, Sharon remains unsure of the boy's origins:

"My husband is convinced that boy was a demon. I'm not sure I even believe in demons but whatever he was, he brought bad luck to us and almost destroyed our family. I just hope people remember these things should be left alone."

Did the black eyed child create the illness and car accident, or was he an omen of the coming upheaval Sharon and her family experienced? The family remains plagued by questions they may never be able to answer.

Omens of Disaster

A growing number of people who have had encounters with BEKs report being plagued with strange mishaps, misfortunes, accidents, and even family deaths in the wake of the children's appearances.

Is this a result of the BEKs themselves imparting some type of negative energy or 'curse'? How and why do the children set such things in motion? Are they simply omens of bad things to come? Whether they are demonic, alien or some other type of entity, one thing is becoming clear, they are a precursor of change for those who encounter them, and the changes are not always good.

Beth's Story

"They're omens of bad luck," Beth told me. She didn't want to speak extensively about her run in with the children; at least, she didn't want to talk about the specifics of the encounter, but she was insistent that after meeting them, her life took a drastic turn for the worse.

"I don't know if they did it themselves or if they just showed up at the same time that some horrible changes started in my life, but the kids and my bad luck are connected. Either way, they had something to do with it. You

see, right after the black eyed kids showed up at my apartment, everything went to hell. My boyfriend of seven years up and left on the same day that I was laid off from my job. All this was the third day after encountering the kids.

The first day after seeing them, I got sick, a really nasty stomach virus. The second day someone broke into my car and stole my laptop. None of that mattered after the third day, when I lost my relationship and my job."

Beth encountered the black eyed kids in a scenario similar to other people. They showed up randomly at her door and insisted on entering her apartment. Wisely, she refused, but the effects of the experience were intense nonetheless.

"So much happened to me that week. I kept trying to put those kids out of my mind but I was reeling from all the loss. I started to wonder if I had imagined them. I kept asking myself if it was all a figment of my imagination. But if it wasn't, did they have something to do with all the horrible things that happened right after?"

Although Beth was reluctant to talk about her experience with the kids, there was one glaring difference in her encounter with the BEKs that I hadn't heard before.

One of them touched her.

"It was the girl. She grabbed my wrist so quick that I didn't even see it happen. She was just holding my wrist all of a sudden. I looked down at her hand resting there. She wasn't gripping me hard, but she was cold, at least, her hand was cold as ice."

Beth insists the children did not enter her house, nor did they do anything else forceful. The touch on her wrist didn't seem like an attempt to hold her, or force her to do anything.

"I just pulled my hand back and went inside. Right after that night though, a lot of bad things started happening."

After seeing the kids, Beth had a restless evening and couldn't get to sleep. It was just the beginning. The sleepless night was followed by her illness, the theft from her car, and then the loss of her job and boyfriend. She was an emotional wreck by the end of the week.

"I don't normally do this, but I went to a psychic. My mother uses them all the time and she got me an appointment with one she thought was especially good. I went to see this woman and I was a wreck. It was just a

week after my encounter with the children and less than a week since my boyfriend had left me. I figured she couldn't tell me anything that would be any worse than what had already happened."

Beth was apprehensive about the session, and says she was careful to reveal nothing to the psychic.

"I'm a little skeptical about these things; I knew that she would probably start in about my being in an emotional state. I'm sure that anyone could have figured that out with the physical condition that I was in. Sure enough, she started saying that she sensed that I had suffered loss. I felt like getting up and leaving, I really didn't want anyone telling me it was all okay, or for the better, or any kind of psychobabble. All of a sudden though, she stopped. This was maybe ten minutes into the session. I hadn't said a word the whole time, just stated my name for her. She not only stopped talking, but her face flushed and then she looked pale all of a sudden like the blood had drained out of her face. It must have been for a couple of minutes or so, she didn't say anything and I just waited."

Beth said the psychic's demeanor changed drastically when she spoke next.

"It was as if she was dropping her act. She looked straight at me and asked me if I knew what those things that I saw were."

Beth knew what the psychic was talking about, but she didn't want to voice it herself. She tried to act normal and asked a question herself.

"What is it? What things? What are you seeing?"

"The psychic looked scared," Beth said. *"She said to me, "You ran into two kids, a boy and a girl. Their eyes were solid black and I believe they cursed you."*

Beth couldn't believe what she was hearing. In her mind, a psychic could take wild guesses and get a few things right, filling in the rest with nonsense. There was no way this woman would have thought up an encounter with black eyed kids. Beth hadn't even told her mother about seeing the children.

The woman shook her head and stood up.

"There's nothing I can do for you dear," the psychic told Beth. *"You need to see a priest or something."*

The psychic told Beth she would issue a refund for the reading and promptly escorted her out.

"She did suggest a few different people that I could contact but she made it clear she couldn't do anything and that she wanted me to leave."

"I can't risk those things showing up here," the psychic told Beth. *"You go get some help."*

Beth later sought out a spiritual figure she was comfortable with for counseling and a blessing. She reports that, after the blessing, her life began to improve. She won't talk about the black eyed children much, as she's convinced that if she starts to focus on them, they may return to her door.

Suspicious Minds

Beth is one of a growing number of people who have contacted me regarding the 'curse' of the BEKs. Car accidents, illnesses, both short and long-term, loss of employment, and drastic changes in personal relationships, have all been attributed to encounters with black eyed kids.

Are the black eyed children really capable of creating troubling events in a person's life? Lest these ideas sound too far-fetched, we must consider the mental and emotional effect these children have on the people who encounter them. If a witness believes the children are a bad omen, then that is exactly what they will be in that person's life.

Superstitions still carry a lot of power, even in the modern age. Thousands of people still go out of their way to avoid walking under ladders, or allowing a black cat to cross their path. If ever there was a symbol that looked like an ominous sign of bad luck, the black eyed kids certainly fit the bill.

Indeed, many people believe talking about or even thinking about the black eyed children too much will 'call them forth' and create another encounter. The implication is that the BEKs are 'tuned in' to the vibration created by studying them. Pay too much attention to them, and they'll return the favor. It may be a curious argument, but again, it may be related to a level of energy connection most people don't fully understand. In the not too distant past, people believed talking or thinking about the devil would call him forth. The principle is the same as the common experience of thinking about a friend or relative and having them phone out of the blue. A manifestation of the collective, as Jung would say.

Perhaps the black eyed kids are aware on an energetic level. If this is the case, then energy focused on them, be it thought or conversation, may provoke a response from them.

Of course, there is the possibility the kids transmit some kind of kinetic energy that sets things in motion beyond our scope of understanding. The mere act of delaying someone from going inside their house could cause a phone call to be missed, which could lead to another delay and on and on. A domino effect if you will, that could create varying levels of change in the life of those being delayed by the kids.

It may all sound very esoteric but we must consider all possibilities in terms of these beings. If they are truly responsible, to any degree, for misfortune or bad luck, then we should seek to understand exactly what we are dealing with and how best to overcome it.

Harbingers of Death

While most victims of the BEKs merely have unpleasant encounters that haunt them to some degree, there have been others who have fared far worse after seeing the kids. As if periods of bad luck and misfortune were not terrible enough, there is also the possibility the black eyed children are indicators of something much worse. Death.

For thousands of years, people have told tales of menacing figures in black that have come calling to claim the souls of the recently departed. In many stories, the figure is death itself personified in physical form, bringing the touch that ends life. While it does not seem the children themselves are deadly, their appearance may indicate that death is about to befall someone close to the witness.

Paranormal entities as harbingers of doom is certainly not a new idea. The infamous Mothman is the best example of a strange creature, sighted by many people, that appeared prior to a disaster. The Mothman was a giant bird-like creature sighted by numerous people in the Point Pleasant area of West Virginia.

The Mothman was described as being seven feet tall, with a ten-foot wingspan, and large, glowing, red eyes. Numerous witnesses reported frightening encounters with the creature during the brief period of sightings. The culmination of these accounts came on December 15, 1967. That fateful day, the Silver Bridge collapsed resulting in the deaths of forty-six people. Reportedly, sightings of the Mothman ceased in the aftermath of the catastrophe. Many people believe the creature was an omen of the disaster that befell the area.

To this day, there is controversy as to the nature of the Mothman. Arguments to explain the Mothman's origin range from an unidentified cryptid, to an alien being, or a demonic creature. Sounds familiar.

If, like the Mothman, the black eyed children are precursors of disaster, then it seems they operate on a more personal level. There has yet to be a reported incident of black eyed children being encountered prior to a large-scale disaster. There have, however, been several reports of encounters with the BEKs that were followed by family tragedies. Take the case of Charles.

Charles lives outside of New Orleans, Louisiana. He encountered the black eyed kids one night after coming home from a late night with friends:

"My friend dropped me off; I think it was about two in the morning. We stayed out later sometimes but I had to work early the next day. I had him drop me at the end of the block, my house ain't too far down and it made it so he could just keep heading home himself. I walked a few steps and I hear a kid's voice calling out, "Hey mister."

I turned around and sure enough, there was a young kid standing right there behind me. He was close, too, and I don't know how I didn't hear him come up on me, or why I didn't see him when I got out of the car. I looked around since I wanted to make sure it wasn't some funny business, I didn't want any gangbangers coming out at me or something.

I says to him, "What you out here so late for kid?"

He didn't even answer that, just said to me, "Why don't you ask me to walk along with you?"

Now, New Orleans has got some weird things, crime, voodoo, and all types of odd people, but this was a kid, just a kid maybe ten or twelve years old. Why was he acting so strange? I was really kind of afraid to look at him. The streetlights were on, but it was really hard to see much of his features. I'll say this though, the boy had very white skin and maybe it was the streetlight, but it had a funny cast to it. He stood there staring at me with his arms hanging at his sides, it didn't look natural.

Me, I don't want nothing to do with no voodoo or any kind of drug dealings, anything else I just like to stick to myself, do my job and listen to good music. I will tell you, I was afraid of that boy right then. I just turned around and walked away from him and I was walking fast.

I didn't even answer him, but I heard him still talking behind me and I could hear what he said. He says "That's bad, that's bad. You're gonna be sorry you didn't listen to me."

I didn't know what that meant. I just got myself home and locked the doors. I turned the lights off and I got in bed. I just wanted to forget all about it. I couldn't figure out why a kid made me feel so scared."

Charles didn't sleep too long. He was jolted awake at five AM by the telephone. It was his mother calling him to tell him that his sister had passed away.

"She was healthy and we couldn't understand it. The doctors said that she had a heart attack in her sleep and that she went in the middle of the night. I don't know why, but right then I thought about that boy that I had seen on the street and the strange way he acted."

Charles called his work and took the day off so he could go to his mother's house and spend time with family. In the course of the day, he couldn't get his mind off the encounter with the strange boy. He finally told his mother about the incident.

"You done been crossed Charles," she said. *"That was a spirit you saw and it crossed you with something."*

Charles's mother was a devout Christian, but having grown up in Louisiana, she knew much about Voodoo, Hoodoo and the spirit world. She believed the child had 'crossed' her son. In Hoodoo terms, this meant Charles had been cursed.

Charles's mother immediately retrieved her Bible and began to pray over her son. After a series of blessings, she made Charles promise to read certain passages from the Bible over the course of the week.

"I felt better after she prayed over me. We talked about it, and she called her brother in and told him what had happened. He said the same thing, that

I had seen a spirit and that it was a sign of my sister's death. We all prayed that no other deaths would come, and that no more bad luck would harm any of the family."

Charles reports he had trouble sleeping in the weeks following his encounter on the street. He avoided walking the block late at night, not wanting to take any chance, or risk seeing the boy again.

"One time was enough for me. If he was a spirit he was as real as you and I, but I don't want to see one ever again. I don't know what it had to do with my sister's death, but I know the two are connected. I still read from the Bible every night, and I'm thankful that nothing else has happened to my family.

I think those kids are something evil and I know what to do if they come around again. They can't do any more harm as long as I have my faith and as long as I stay strong if I have to confront them."

Charles is not the only person to contact me regarding a death in the family after an encounter with the black eyed children. Fortunately, the number of such reports is very small by comparison. I hope such reports will continue to be the exception rather than the rule.

Lauren's Story

The fear the children create in witnesses is another thing that seems to linger long after their appearance. Many people who encounter the beings are afraid to talk at length about their experience because they fear more ill fortune. They believe focusing on the children may cause them to return. Some witnesses, in fact, feel the BEKs still follow them after the initial encounter, lurking in the shadows and waiting for another opportunity to reveal themselves.

Lauren relates her experience of the aftermath of a visit by the BEKs:

"I've seen them several times since my close encounter with them. It was at a distance, but I know it was them. The first time was two days after they originally showed up at my door.

I walked to the store a few blocks away to get some bread and a couple of other items. All the way there I kept having a strange feeling, you know the feeling you have when you think someone is watching you. When I would look around though, there was nothing there so I thought it was my imagination. I walk my neighborhood all the time and I'd never had such a nervous feeling before. On the way back home, the feeling was worse, much more intense. I was convinced that I was being followed, or watched. It was terrible feeling so paranoid.

There were a few other people out walking and I probably gave them strange looks. I couldn't wait to get home. I was halfway there when I noticed them. Across the street, there was a cluster of three big trees. I stopped and looked over at those trees, I just had a feeling. Then I saw them, the same two boys that had shown up at my door. They were standing, halfway behind the tree in the center and they were just staring at me. They were wearing the same clothing as the night I first saw them. I just knew they had been watching me the whole time. I picked up my pace, anxious to get home. When I turned and looked back towards them, they were gone."

Lauren claims the kids showed up on several other occasions. The second time was in the parking lot of her place of employment.

"I was just getting off work. I had worked late and the parking lot was mostly empty when I went to get in my car. I opened the door and had that strange feeling. I stood there by my car with the door opened and looked around. It's a pretty safe neighborhood and the lot is very open. I didn't see anything so I got in my car and started the engine. I pulled out of the parking spot, put the car in drive and started to pull forward. Just then I saw them. They were standing at the corner of the office building. Again, I knew it was the same two boys because they had the same clothing on. I raced out of that lot and got home as quick as I could."

Lauren says the additional sightings of the children were spread out over the course of a couple of weeks. Although she was frightened by the presence of the kids, she didn't feel there was anything she could report to the police. Each time, the kids appeared to vanish very quickly once she noticed them. After yet another sighting of the same kids in a neighborhood park, Lauren decided to try a different tactic.

"I resolved myself to ignoring those boys. I felt like they were getting a kick out of seeing my reactions so I decided I wouldn't give them anything that might satisfy them. There were a few other times that I had that feeling again and I believe they were around, watching me. I just pushed it aside and acted completely normal. After a couple of those kinds of experiences they seemed to have went away."

Like most people who encounter black eyed beings, Lauren is unsure what they are, or what they wanted from her. She's just happy they seem to have finally left her alone.

"I hope that they never come back but to tell you the truth there's always this feeling in the back of my mind that I'll see them again, probably when I least expect it. I'll deal with it the same way. I refuse to let those kids affect me any more than they already have."

Like many other witnesses, Lauren believes the initial encounter with the BEKs allowed them to form a connection to her. She believes that through disciplining herself to ignore them, she forced the connection with the kids to be severed. Although she worries about them returning, she is adamant that if they do, she will continue to ignore them and conduct her life as if they didn't exist. She can't deny they had an influence on her for a time, but through staying positive, she's sure they won't influence her anymore.

The black eyed children have quite an impact on the people who encounter them. Something about the children haunts the minds of witnesses causing them to linger to some degree whether it is in dreams or thoughts. Many others believe the children never really go away but continue to be there, somewhere in the distance, watching and waiting.

PART 3:

Beyond The Children
Black Eyed Entities

Chapter 15

Evil Eyes & Energy Thieves

The black eyed children are certainly one of the strangest topics in the paranormal field today and the study of these encounters has only just begun. While the accounts are unusual, the children share traits with many other supernatural beings from around the world. By looking beyond the black eyed kids, and the obvious associations, such as demons and aliens, perhaps we can gain more understanding and clarity about the nature of these entities.

Some of the most common abilities exhibited by BEKs have roots in much older, paranormal entities. Folklore and historical accounts are filled with beings reputed to have "evil eyes," mind controlling powers, and the ability to drain energy from their victims.

This section contains a brief look at some of these entities. While not a comprehensive list, it is a starting point to further understand the black eyed beings now visiting people around the globe.

From the evil eye of the Jettatore of Italy, to tales of black eyed angels in the Middle East; from energy draining succubi, to Europe's tales of changelings. Many of these creatures have reached mythic proportions and studying them may help us solve the puzzle of the black eyed children.

While there are other, similar creatures to be found in myth and lore, the ones listed here most closely resemble the BEKs on some level. I hope a deeper study of these sinister beings will lead us to more answers about the BEK phenomenon. Ultimately, time, energy and research will give us more insight into the black eyed kid mystery and its origins. Eventually, we may have a clear understanding of what the children want and why they're here.

As you will see, energy thieves come in many forms, and it may be the dark- eyed children themselves are simply a modern version of one of these ancient entities, back to plague us again in a new form.

Chapter 16

Phantoms

There's nothing on the surface to indicate the black eyed children are ghost or spirits. They are reportedly solid in appearance and openly interact with humans who encounter them. Additionally, they are very rarely seen in the same location, which would rule out any kind of residual apparition.

It is curious to note, however, that there are a few incidents of ghosts appearing with black eyes, or no eyes at all.

In the last ten years, there's been a massive increase in ghost sightings around the world. The greater number of these encounters involve strange sounds, phantom voices, or objects that move on their own accord. Although rare, some accounts do report partial or full body apparitions. These 'partial' apparitions are sightings of spirits that are not quite complete. Most frequently, people will report that the phantom image is missing its feet. Sometimes, only a torso, or only a pair of legs is witnessed. On a few occasions, however, the missing component is the eyes.

Take the story of Carlotta who had the ghost of a strange girl without eyes living in her family home.

Carlotta's Story

Carlotta grew up in Boston, Massachusetts. When she was twelve years old, her family moved into a house in a historic neighborhood where many of the homes had a reputation for ghostly activity. Carlotta says her family home was haunted by several spirits including an elderly man, a soldier, and an odd little girl without eyes.

"I was pretty sensitive when I was young and I used to see a lot of things around our house. There was a man who looked older to me, maybe in his sixties, who was always walking or standing around in the front room of the house. The front room was a sitting room and we hardly ever used it for anything. It had some antique furniture my parents had bought, just a small sofa, chair and table. The room was opened to the stairway and I'd see the man pretty often when I was going up or down the steps.

There was the ghost of a soldier too. My brother and I both saw him a couple of times. It was a very old uniform like something from the revolutionary period. I don't think he was American though, he always kind of scared me a little.

The ghost of the little girl was the one I saw the most often. For a long time, I would see her walking in the hallway near the stairs. I wasn't scared of her at all. Whenever I tried to get close, she would just vanish. I finally stopped trying to walk up to her. Instead, I would say hello and pretend to just keep playing. The door to my room was usually standing open and I would see her across the hall, looking towards me and watching what I was doing.

The girl was probably about six or seven years old. She always had the same clothes on, an old-fashioned white dress. Her hair was long and brown, and her skin seemed rather pale, but I could never tell much more about her because she stayed far away."

Carlotta says the pattern remained the same for a couple of years. The spirit of the girl would appear several times close together, then not be seen for a few weeks or more. She never came any closer, preferring to remain in the hallway where she could see into the bedrooms. The pattern changed one chilly fall evening.

"It was cold outside that week. It was late October and the air was crisp. For some reason, my mother had decided to let me have some hot apple cider up in my room. This was rare as she never let me have food or drink upstairs. I was sitting on the floor on a beanbag chair, reading a book. I had the cider

beside me on the floor within arm's reach. I wasn't really paying attention to anything, just my book, when all of a sudden, I felt a cold draft. I looked up and there stood the little girl.

I couldn't believe it. After all that time, she had finally come into my room and I wasn't sure why. She stood there just a couple of feet away and it was the first time that I really got a good look at her. She looked like a normal little girl in every way except for one thing.

She had no eyes.

It scared me and made me curious at the same time. I mean that I didn't feel afraid of the girl, but the lack of eyes was so strange. There weren't any marks or anything, it didn't seem like anything violent had happened to her. There just weren't any eyes where they should have been. All you could see in place of the eyes were dull, black holes.

I didn't say anything and the girl just stood there with her head tilted towards me. After a moment, she leaned over, bending at the waist towards my cup of hot cider. You could see her tilt her nose up like she was taking a good long whiff of that cider. As soon as she did that, she stood back up and promptly vanished."

Carlotta believed the girl she encountered was a ghost. She's sure it was the same spirit she had witnessed countless times in the hallway. The girl had a 'wispy' appearance according to Carlotta, and dissipated, vanishing before her eyes. There was also a shift in temperature when the girl entered the room creating the classic 'cold spot' often experienced by those who witness apparitions.

"I could never understand why that girl didn't have any eyes. I always thought that ghosts looked like they did whenever they died, but I can't see any reason, medical or otherwise, for a living person to look like that, so why did her spirit appear that way?"

Carlotta's case is not completely unique, other people have encountered spirits that seemed to look like normal people in every respect, except for a black void where the eyes would normally be. Assuming they have a choice, it's hard to determine the reason why a spirit would manifest in such a manner. Perhaps there was a trauma involving the eyes before their death. Perhaps the person, when living, was blind and therefore has no reason to display eyes in their spirit form. It's a curious question, and yet another of the many mysteries of what lies beyond death. Whatever the cause, it presents a rather disturbing form to those confronted with the already startling reality of witnessing a ghost.

Another account of such a spirit comes from California.

John and Nathan's Account

John and Nathan call themselves 'amateur ghost hunters.' Inspired by the numerous ghost hunting reality shows on television, they purchased basic equipment and began dabbling in the field as a weekend hobby. On one occasion, they made a trip to a cemetery with a reputation for being haunted and encountered the ghost of a young man without eyes.

"We had heard about this cemetery and that a lot of people had seen weird things there," says John. *"So, we decided we wanted to check it out and do an investigation."*

One sunny afternoon, John and his friend Nathan took a drive out to the cemetery to look the area over and familiarize themselves with the surroundings.

"We intended to get the layout down while it was daylight. Once we knew what all was there we were going to go back in the middle of the night, take our equipment, and see what happened. Hopefully, we could pick up some spirit voices on our recorders (EVPs) or something. I think it's a creepy place, even in broad daylight. Lots of the headstones are really old and you can't even see the dates on all of them due to the erosion of the stones. Parts of the cemetery are overgrown with weeds; it looks like no one's really taking care of the place. It has a fence around it, but the gate hangs open and parts of the fence have fallen over.

It's a little out of the way and I know some other ghost hunters have been there to investigate, so we weren't the first. Mostly though, it gets teenagers going out there at night who want to drink beer, party and scare their girlfriends. We walked around the whole area, just checking things out. This was about three thirty in the afternoon so there was still plenty of light. Nathan was bending down, trying to see the dates on a really old headstone. I had walked a few feet away, looking off at the area surrounding the cemetery. I had a video camera but I wasn't filming anything yet, I wanted to just walk around first.

There was this big tree towards one side of the cemetery. It was actually inside the rusted fence and there were a couple of old headstones under the shade of the tree. All of a sudden, I realized that there was a man standing there, under the branches of the tree. I thought this was maybe a caretaker or something because he had on what looked like work clothes to me. Just a simple dark blue shirt and work pants. He was looking right at me, so I said something to him.

"Hey, how you doing?"

He didn't respond and I was still taking steps towards him. I stopped walking because I had a funny feeling. I stood there looking and realized this guy wasn't moving a muscle. All the hair went up on the back of my neck. Right at that moment, Nathan approached from my right side. He got up next to me and looked over at the man by the tree. It was just dawning on me that I was seeing a ghost. I looked down at his legs, and you couldn't see any feet. The legs sort of faded away past the knees.

Nathan said in a low tone, "He doesn't have any eyes".

I looked up at the man's face and realized Nathan was right. Where the eyes should have been, there were only two black holes, as black as you can imagine. The odd thing is, I know that man was 'looking' directly at us.

I think we were both frozen in place. I had a camera in my hand and I never once thought about raising it up and taking a picture. I think I was even holding my breath. And the man, well, one minute he was there and the next minute he was gone. He disappeared completely. I turned and looked at Nathan but neither of us could say anything. We got in the car and left. We didn't go back that night either."

It took John and Nathan a while to come to terms with having witnessed the full apparition of a ghost. They returned to the cemetery two weeks later, with a couple of friends in tow. However, there was no evidence of the specter on their return and they discovered that the headstones under the tree were too weathered to read any of the information.

"We kind of thought, maybe there'd be a name on one of those stones, and it might be the guy we saw. Who knows though, his clothing didn't look old enough to match those headstones. Either way, the whole experience was just too creepy for us. It's one thing to see ghost hunters on TV hearing noises and stuff. We never expected to actually see a ghost. That guy, I won't say he was evil, but there was just something wrong with him not having any eyes. For now, we're done with ghost hunting as a hobby. Once we get over that encounter, we'll probably try it again but seeing that ghost is a hard thing to forget about."

Why the big increase in reports of ghosts and hauntings? The fact is, reports of all manner of strange creatures, unidentified objects, and other strange manifestations are on the rise. This is partially due to the tremendous popularity of the paranormal. The paranormal craze shows no signs of going away, movies, television shows, books, and magazines about paranormal topics are more popular than ever. With this popularity people have become more comfortable reporting their own strange encounters.

There are other factors involved too. The change in people's attitudes toward the paranormal goes deeper than a willingness to watch popular television shows. People, more than ever, now WANT to experience something paranormal. While it could be argued that this mindset causes a lot of mistaken identifications, we must also consider that people have become more open to an awareness of the strange and weird. Accepting, on some level, that there is more to the world than we understand allows more opportunities for the strange to manifest.

A global shift in consciousness is leading to a greater interest in the mysteries of the world around us and greater curiosity about what lies beyond the normal nine-to-five world. As humans increase their awareness, the possibilities expand rapidly. This simple but powerful shift is leading to greater numbers of people having close encounters with beings beyond our day-to-day reality.

Chapter I7

The Evil Eye

It is the most widespread superstition in the world. Versions of it can be found across Europe, the Americas, and parts of Africa and Asia.

It can bring misery, misfortune and terrible illness.

It may come as a stare, a lingering look or even a quick glance.

It is known as 'The Evil Eye.'

Power of the Evil Eye

It has long been believed that when someone with the evil eye looks at a person, animal or even an object while dwelling on negative thoughts or feelings, a curse is transmitted. Expressions of envy, greed and anger are just a few of the negative energies that can power the evil eye. It is the look itself that sends the curse from the eyes into the target being stared at. It's said even a lingering look is enough to cast the eye's energy. An intentional casting of the evil eye can carry much power, but many cultures profess the energy of the evil eye can often be sent unintentionally. Within these beliefs, anyone can cast the evil eye simply by looking at someone or something with jealousy or desire. Admiring a friend's new clothes, or a couple's new baby, becomes risky with such possibilities. While it may be unintentional, the effects from this type of evil eye are no less powerful. Indeed, a lingering gaze from someone sending the evil eye can make the skin crawl and create sickness, misfortune, and, in extreme cases, death.

History of the Evil Eye

The dreaded evil eye has roots far back in history. The Sumerians, Babylonians and Assyrians all mentioned it repeatedly. The ancient Egyptians feared it and writings of many early cultures warn against the dangers of the curse's power. Modern Christians, Jews and Arabs all acknowledge the evil eye and it's mentioned several times in the Bible, for instance these passages from Proverbs:

"Eat thou not the bread of him that hath an evil eye, neither desire thou his dainty meat." Proverbs 23:6

"He that hasteneth to be rich hath an evil eye and considereth not that poverty shall come upon him." Proverbs 28:22

The ancient Greeks and Romans were also aware of the power of the evil eye. Roman historian and writer Plutarch believed there was a scientific explanation for the eye's power. He stated that the eyes were the source of deadly rays that could spring up like poisoned darts from the inner recesses of a person possessing the evil eye. The Romans believed that among some tribes, all members possessed the power to cast the evil eye. The tribes of Scythia and Pontus were especially noted for this ability.

Much like the witch hunts of the past, reclusive people, and those without children or families, were often scapegoats in communities looking for supernatural causes of their misfortunes. Women who were unable to bear children were often suspected of having the power of the evil eye. This is likely due to people believing they were exhibiting jealousy towards those with babies. A passing glance at a newborn from a childless woman would cause immediate suspicion and fear. In ancient times, infant mortality rates were high and the evil eye was often blamed. This reinforced the belief that babies, young children, and pregnant women were especially vulnerable to the power of the eye. Special care had to be taken, lest they fall victim to its power. No one was considered immune to this mystical force, however. Men, animals and even objects could all suffer from being a target of the evil eye.

A wide variety of symptoms and conditions can indicate one has been afflicted by this ancient evil. Accidents, bad luck, problems with relationships and careers are all indicators of having been cursed. A lack of focus and low mental energy can be due to the evil eye, and a long list of physical difficulties may arise. These include headaches, stomach cramps, diarrhea, vomiting, fevers and cold sweats. A loss of sleep and appetite may also result from having the evil eye cast on you.

In ancient times, it was believed the evil eye could dry up the milk from cows, the juice of fruit trees, and even the milk created by a nursing mother. The evil eye could also cause a man to lose his potency by 'drying' him up.

It would seem the threat of physically drying up and withering away is the very root of the fears generated by the evil eye. Professor Alan Dundes of the University of California at Berkeley theorizes the true evil done by the gaze of the evil eye was related to dehydration. Writing in *The Evil Eye: A Casebook,* his study of the subject, he contends the focus on dehydration demonstrates that the origins of the evil eye come from the deserts of the Middle East.

The evil eye was not quite as serious in some parts of Europe. In old Scottish, the word for the evil eye translates as 'overlooking' implying that a person has lingered too long in admiring an object or person. This long look is likely envious; hence it causes the curse of the evil eye to be sent into the admired object or person.

But unlike in Scotland, the evil eye gained a solid foothold in the Mediterranean. Belief in its power has always been especially strong in Italy where the power of the eye is referred to as "Malocchio" (pronounced: mal-oak-yo). In Italy, the evil eye is often associated with Stregheria, traditional Italian witchcraft and sorcery. The Strega, or female witch, was sometimes thought to have the ability to cast the evil eye at will.

The 'mano cornuta' or 'horned hand' gesture, developed in Italy as a defense against the evil eye. The gesture is made by holding up the first finger and pinky finger while the thumb and two middle fingers are folded inward toward the palm. The horned hand gesture became very popular in the United States due to its use by heavy metal rock bands. Ronnie James Dio was one of the first to bring it to popularity while he was a front man for the rock group Black Sabbath. Dio himself claims he learned the gesture from his Italian grandmother.

In an amusing twist, most rock and roll fans seem to believe the symbol represents the devil and the power of Satan. Little do the rocking masses know they are warding off the evil eye while banging their heads.

Many Italian-Americans are well versed in stories of the power of the evil eye, various signs of the curse, and the proper ways to defend against it. Amulets in the form of the horned hand have also long been used to ward off the evil eye.

Cristina's Story

Cristina is an Italian-American now living in New York City. I spoke with her at length about the BEKs and the evil eye to learn more about possible connections. Cristina's grandparents grew up in the Italian countryside and her family comes from a long line of practitioners of traditional Italian folk magic.

"When we were kids, we were taught about the evil eye, how to watch out for it, what the signs were if you were afflicted by it, and what to do about it. We were taught to make the 'mano cornuto,' what you know as the horned hand sign. We were also taught a prayer that we should recite right away if we saw the evil eye or even suspected that someone had it. Its power was not to be laughed at. My grandfather also gave each of us kids a little stone, like a marble with blue and white stripes on it. We were told to keep it with us all the time because it would ward off the power of the evil eye."

According to Cristina, she was taught the evil eye can be cast intentionally or by accident. Either way, the effect can be quite damaging and disaster can follow. Vomiting, shakes, accidents and great misfortune can all result. If the eye is malicious and has enough power, it can even lead to death.

Although Cristina has not seen the black eyed children herself, she believes, based on the stories, that they are bearers of the evil eye and have been around for a long time.

"I was always taught that you watched out for anyone who had eyes that were either black, red or bright blue in color. I know a lot of people don't believe that someone can have red eyes, but I have seen it once before.

My family taught me that any of these unusual colors would be a mark that the person had the power to cast the evil eye. You are not supposed to make eye contact with them. If they stare at you too long, or if you feel strange when they glance at you, then you must take measures to remove any evil that was placed on you."

Cristina related a story passed on to her by her grandmother. It dealt with a strange child who visited her grandmother's village:

"My grandmother told me that back in Italy, when she was a young woman, there was a black eyed child that some people saw around her village. No one knew where this child came from because he was not from there and everyone knew all the children in town. They thought perhaps he was lost, that he had wandered away from his family somehow, or come from a nearby village.

He was seen over the course of three days by many different people. Some tried to help him, to ask him questions, but they couldn't get any answers from him. Everyone was worried because they said he had the evil eye. His eyes were black. I don't know if they were solid black or not, but everyone talked about the boy having black eyes.

My grandmother said that people who tried to talk to the boy became sick very suddenly. For three days in a row different people saw him and suddenly he was gone. After that, he never came back. The people in the village took measures to remove the curse and they all eventually recovered."

Defense Against the Evil Eye

Various eye symbols are used to defend against the effects of the evil eye. The eye of Buddha, the Egyptian eye of Horus, and even stones and small gems resembling eyes are all considered protective charms against the power of the evil eye.

Other methods to protect oneself against the evil eye are as varied as the cultures that believe in its power. Over the years, countless defenses have been created to neutralize it. Horseshoes are one such method. Nailed over doorways, the horseshoe is said to prevent the power of the eye, or those who carry it, from entering the home.

Red cords are another popular tool to defend against the influence of the eye; these are worn on the wrist or around the neck. Many people still tie a red cord around the wrist of infants who are particularly vulnerable to the power of the eye. Numerous amulets are fashioned in the shape of an eye, or often a hand with an eye imbedded in the palm. These amulets can be found in markets around the world.

In some areas, mirrors are sewn into garments as a protection. It's believed mirrors will reflect the evil eye back at the person who sends it.

When the belief in the evil eye made it to the Americas, the tradition found a foothold among many of the indigenous peoples, especially in Central and South America. The evil eye and its effects became well known in Mexico and across the American southwest. Among the Hispanics of the region, folk cures to conquer the eye's influence include a rich blend of traditional magic and Catholic symbolism. The sign of the cross is often utilized, traced over the body, or physically worn as a protection. Eggs are also used to absorb the curse from the body and spirit of those afflicted.

Writing in her book, *"The Healer Of Los Olmas And Other Mexican Lore"* author Soledad Perez recounts the tale of a woman who believed her child became afflicted by the gaze of the evil eye.

This story about the girl "Chita," portrays some of the common symptoms associated with an evil eye affliction, including a very high fever. Chita's condition does not improve until a family friend recognizes what is wrong and applies a folk remedy to remove the 'curse' affecting the young child.

Chita's Curse

"When Chita was small, I took her downtown on one occasion. She was a pretty little girl and people admired her. While I was standing at the counter of one of the department stores, a little Mexican woman approached me and wanted to touch Chita.

She said, "What a pretty baby! Won't you let me touch her hair and eyes?"

I didn't like for people to be touching the baby so I said, "No, please don't touch her!"

The little woman left and I didn't believe in the evil eye so I thought no more about it.

The next day Chita became ill. She had a very high fever and was flushed and uneasy. I called the doctor. He came and looked at her. Two or three days went by and Chita didn't improve. She just seemed to get worse. We went from one doctor to another but it didn't do any good.

Finally, one day my comrade Mrs. Ramos came over and she looked at Chita and said, "This child is suffering from the evil eye. I can cure her if you will let me try."

I told her to go ahead and she did. She asked for two eggs and a cup. One of the eggs she passed over Chita's whole face. Then she took the egg, broke it, put it in a cup, stirred it, and made a cross with some of it on Chita's forehead. While doing this she pronounced several prayers. The egg she placed on the mantelpiece in the living room and asked that no one touch it.

The next day Mrs. Ramos came back. Chita's fever was gone and you could tell she was better. Mrs. Ramos then took the egg from the mantelpiece and broke it. If I hadn't been there, I wouldn't believe it, but my husband and I both saw it. The egg looked as if it were hard-boiled.

Mrs. Ramos said, "Chita will get well now. The evil eye has gone into the egg; that's why it looks like this."

Chita got well.

What is the truth of the evil eye? Is it simply an ancient superstition or a genuine power we still don't understand? For thousands of people around the world, it is a dark reality. A true evil that must be guarded against at each turn. Even in our modern world, cultures around the globe carry on traditions of cures and protections against this ancient power. It may be a simple, outdated belief. Then again, confronting a child with solid black eyes could make anyone believe in occult powers.

Jettatores

In Sicily, there are tales of the Jettatore, men said to be born with eyes that can damage anything they gaze upon. They are regarded with respect and awe and they are not to be crossed. "Where the Jettatore goes, there he is feared."

While it's believed anyone can cast the evil eye, often without intending to, the Jettatore have a special ability. They are considered 'projectors' or 'throwers,' and they are born with the ability to control the evil eye and its power. The willpower and mind of the Jettatore directs the energy of his eyes, casting the evil glance on anyone or anything he chooses to curse.

Although modern Italy is primarily a Christian nation, the roots of the region are rich in pagan and magical traditions. Belief in the power of the evil eye, or 'malocchio' is still strong, especially in the Italian countryside and on the island of Sicily.

Since malocchio is often cast unintentionally by those who look at things with envy or jealousy in their hearts, those who cast the evil eye in this way are almost always filled with remorse, saddened by any ill fortune they have caused. Folk traditions have many remedies for this kind of evil eye affliction, and most people are aware of the proper steps to take to affect a cure before any great illness falls upon them.

The Jettatore, however, are unique.

A Jettatore is always male, and is described as having very striking facial features. Most often, he is a tall, thin man who attracts attention wherever he goes. His black eyes gaze out from under high arching brows. His powerful stare can cast the evil eye on those he gazes upon. It's believed many Jettatore involve themselves with dark magical traditions in an effort to gain additional power. Indulging in forbidden practices, it is said, brings them additional abilities, and further empowers the strength of their evil eye. Men who are particularly successful, or who exhibit unusual charisma, often gain notoriety as a Jettatore. Historical figures from gangsters to popes have been reported to have the power of the Jettatore's eyes.

If one meets the eyes of a Jettatore, great misfortune could ensue as they are not to be crossed. Illness or bad luck can follow if such a gaze is cast upon you.

One of the best and most well-known protections against the Jettatore's evil eye is the amulet known as the 'cornicello,' or 'little horn.' The horn is a general symbol of good luck in Italy and specifically protects the wearer against the power of the evil eye. The horn itself is a long, gently twisted horn that likely started out as a fertility symbol. The cornicello is traditionally carved from red coral, but in later years, it began to be available in precious metals. Gold and silver are now the most common versions of the talisman. They can be found in markets and jewelry stores around the world. Most people who purchase it merely believe it's a decorative piece of jewelry inspired by Italian design. In reality, they are buying protection against an ancient evil.

His Holiness, The Jettatore

Pope Pius IX was head of the Catholic Church from 1846 until his death in 1878. His reign lasted for thirty-one and a half years, making him the longest ruling pope in history. Some people were frightened of Pius because they feared his evil eye. In fact, some still attribute his long reign as pope to the power of his so-called 'evil eyes.'

While he is often referred to as a Jettatore, he is not considered to have been a malicious man. More often, it's believed he had the 'unfortunate' power of the evil eye and that he inadvertently cursed both people and places.

It seems, during Pius's reign, disasters regularly befell both people and places the pope blessed. This, of course, caused many people to pray they would NOT be blessed by pope Pius. His treatment of the Jews was especially bad during the latter portion of his time in office, and several controversies arose over political choices he made regarding the Jewish people living in Rome.

Another Pius Jettatore

Oddly enough, another Pope Pius is considered by some to have been a Jettatore. Sometimes called the 'Nazi Pope,' Pope Pius XII reigned from 1939 until 1958, encompassing the years of World War II. Although he was not blamed for numerous disasters at the time, many people feel he had Malocchio, and that he turned a blind eye to the Holocaust, the plight of the Jews, and the acts of the Axis powers.

History has not favored Pope Pius XII, as many people believe he could have done more to stop Adolf Hitler and the spread of Fascism in Germany and Italy. At the least, it is felt he could have done more to assist the plight of the Jews.

Did these popes really carry the curse, or the power, of the Jettatore? At the least, it's certainly an odd coincidence that Jews suffered under the rule of two Popes named Pius, who were both reputed to have the power of the evil eye within their control.

Other Jettatore

The list of men considered Jettatore is long and winds its way through some of history's most notable figures. Members of the house of Borgia, prominent during the Renaissance, are reputed to have been Jettatore. In modern times, leaders such as Adolf Hitler and Benito Mussolini are pointed to as examples of Jettatore who used the gaze of their evil eye to control and dominate the masses. These men, not content with personal power, chose to release the magic of their curse on the world.

While a Jettatore's eyes can be any shade, black and bright blue are considered the strongest colors for this magical ability. Startling colors having a 'piercing' gaze and are to be especially feared.

Chapter 18

Dark Angels

Angels appear in a wide variety of guises, from small cherubs and children, to the more common, adult-sized beings with human-like guises and feathered wings. Religious texts describe a wide range of characteristics these heavenly beings display, and amidst the vast number of angels, there are a few that are, at least at times, depicted with black eyes.

The Angels of Judgment

Munkar and Nakir

There are two black eyed angels found in the Muslim belief system. They are known in Arabic as Munkar and Nakir, which translates as 'the denied' and 'the denier.' Munkar and Nakir are not mentioned by name in the Quran, the Muslim holy book. They are, however, mentioned several times in the Hadith, a sacred text that holds almost equal weight with the Quran among many Muslims.

In Islamic tradition, these two angels are sent to test the faith of the dead in their graves. Many Muslims believe that, after death, the soul continues to exist in the grave. Believers call this stage of the afterlife 'barzakh.' It's during this period that Munkar and Nakir visit the deceased. When the funeral rites are complete and the last member of the funeral congregation is forty paces away from the grave, the angels arrive. Munkar and Nakir then prop the body of the deceased's soul upright in his grave and ask the spirit three questions:

Who is your lord?

Who is your prophet?

What is your religion?

A righteous believer will answer without hesitation replying that their lord is Allah, their prophet is Muhammad, and their religion is Islam.

If the deceased answers all three questions correctly, they will enjoy a pleasant time awaiting the resurrection. There is rejoicing, and the soul is taken gently from the body and carried off to enjoy a period in paradise.

If, however, the answers given by the deceased are not correct, the spirit will suffer terrible punishment until the Day of Judgment. The soul is treated as an infidel and the severe punishment includes being beaten on the head by iron clubs. The infidel's soul is then painfully ripped from the body and carried off to suffer torments.

The soul's meeting with Munkar and Nakir is considered a Muslim's greatest trial after death. Family members take great care to place the corpse in the ground facing Mecca. They then pray for the deceased to find success in his trial.

It is considered vital that the last thing a Muslim hears at the time of death is the declaration of faith. Hearing this declaration, it is believed, will assist the soul in remembering his faith so the spirit is not vulnerable to evil in the afterlife and during the trial.

There are varying descriptions of Munkar and Nakir. Some accounts claim the pair have solid black eyes and a shoulder-span measured in miles. It's said when they speak tongues of fire issue from their mouths. Their voices are said to be as loud as thunder. They bear hammers so large that if all of humankind tried together to move one a single inch they would fail. Other descriptions of the pair of angels claim they have smooth, jet black bodies with either solid black, or piercing blue eyes.

Angels of Death

For centuries, death has been personified as a human-like figure in cultures around the world. Portrayals of death range from India's Yama riding a black buffalo and lassoing souls of the dead, to Yanluo the Chinese god of death who wears traditional robes and a judge's cap. While most cultures depict the figure of death as a man, there are exceptions. The Hindus believe the reaper can take the form of a child, and in Norway, death comes as Pesta, the plague hag, a frightening old woman.

The Grim Reaper is depicted as a skeletal form wrapped in a long, flowing robe and carrying a large scythe with which to "reap" the souls of the dead, whether they are willing to go or not. The grim reaper has become a popular pop culture image, but few people have any idea where the depiction originally came from.

It's likely the grim reaper evolved from earlier legends of the angel of death because of cultural beliefs and fears of death itself. It was in the fifteenth century that Death, the entity, evolved into the now familiar grim reaper. The image has changed little since that time, and he is still depicted as a skeletal, scythe-bearing entity. The figure can be seen in popular fantasy art, on album covers and even t-shirts.

Azrael, the archangel of death manifests as a much more palatable figure, usually appearing as a dark-eyed angel in human form but with large black wings and a dark flowing robe. Many people around the world report encounters with the death angel.

Azrael, the Archangel of Death

"I met the angel of death," claims Lia. "He wears a black robe, it looks like black silk and it shimmers. He has the wings of an angel, they are feathered, but they are black too. His face is that of a gentle, handsome man but his eyes are solid black, not a sign of any other color. They are as black as the night and it feels as though you could lose yourself in them. They shine and it made me think of the night sky when I saw them."

I was sitting in a coffee shop, listening to Lia tell her tale. It's a difficult one for her to relate, and to tell the truth, it's a difficult one to listen to. Although she talked about having met the angel, or rather, the archangel of death, the story is really about her grandparents, and

189

you can feel the emotion in the air when she told her story.

"I had gone to Italy to be with my grandparents. My grandmother had been very sick and we didn't think she would live much longer. I had been very close to her most of my life and I wanted to be there when she passed. A part of me couldn't bear the thought of being there for her death, but I knew it would be worse if I didn't get a chance to say goodbye. I wanted to be there for my grandfather too. They had been together for so many years, and he was always saying he didn't want to live without her in his life, so how could I not go?"

Lia was still saddened by the events that took her to Italy that summer, even though when we met it had been seven years since her fateful journey; but the memory lingered, as did the loss she suffered.

"You see, my parents both died in an accident when I was young, so I never really knew them. As a result, it was my grandparents who were always there for me. They were my father's parents, both full-blooded Italian. They guided me through the ups and downs from childhood to adulthood. I think it made me a very different person, with old-fashioned morals. My grandparents were from such a different generation, and they taught me old-school values that I believe a lot of people my age just don't have. I grew up very spiritual too. They were both devout Catholics and they raised me in the same faith. My grandmother though, she knew all the old folk remedies, everything from how to heal a sore throat, to cures for the evil eye.

I couldn't stand the thought of being without them, but those last few years, they kept talking about how tired they were and how God would call them soon."

Lia fidgeted with her coffee cup, anxiously sliding the cardboard sleeve off and on. It was apparently joyous and painful for her to talk about her grandparents. I picked our cups up and got refills, allowing her the time she needed to continue.

We talked about her grandfather and his knack for fixing things, her grandmother who read passages from the Bible —as if they were cure-alls— whenever Lia was upset or faced life's challenges.

She eventually came back around to the summer of her grandmother's illness.

"By the time I got over there, she was in pretty bad shape. The doctors couldn't really do much for her. One evening I was sitting there by her bedside, and she took my hand, telling me to be strong, and that she would

continue to watch over me after she passed. I had no doubt that she would, but letting go was very hard. It was everything I could do to hold on, trying to be strong and not break down in front of her.

She fell asleep just after that. I sat at her bedside for a bit. Then I got up and went to the kitchen to make coffee. I wasn't sleepy, but it gave me something to do. I had finally talked my grandfather into going to bed to get some rest. He had been staying by her side constantly and I could see how worn out he was.

Even though it was very late, I was determined to stay busy myself. I checked on my grandmother constantly; I wanted to be there for her, for anything that she needed. I didn't want to watch television or listen to music because I wanted to be able to hear her if she called out."

Lia took a long drink of her coffee, her eyes tearing up as she told the story, but she pushed forward.

"An hour or two later, I suddenly jumped up. I had been sitting in a chair in the living room and I guess I fell asleep. It was still dark outside but the room had a lot of light. We had a little altar set up near the door and it was covered in candles. They were all lit, some by us, some by friends who would stop by and offer prayers for my grandmother's health. I had a cup of coffee sitting on the table beside me and it was cold when I reached over to it. I realized then that I must have been asleep longer than I thought. I went in right away and checked on my grandmother. She was sleeping soundly. I went over close enough that I could hear her breathing, just so I could be sure that she was still okay.

I walked back out to the living area. I busied myself, determined to stay awake this time. I didn't even want to sit down again. I made fresh coffee and had drank almost a full cup when I heard a strange sound. I stood there in the middle of the living room listening to it. It was a very gentle rapping. It seems strange, but I just couldn't tell where it was coming from. It felt like it was all around me. I thought it was coming from the walls, the floor, the ceiling, but not all at the same time. It was as though it moved about so you couldn't determine its origin. Finally, I turned and faced the entrance of the house. In that moment, I knew that the knocking was coming from the front door."

Lia became more animated, recalling the events that transpired that night as though they had happened yesterday.

"I walked over and stood facing the door. I was right by the altar and all the candlelight made it very bright.

I just stood there and heard the soft rapping coming from the front door. It stopped and slowly the door opened. I wasn't afraid. I'm not sure what it was that I was feeling to tell you the truth. It sounds crazy, but I just felt comfortable with what was happening. It was like that state you get in sometimes where you've just gotten out of bed, yet you're still in a semi-dream state.

The door swung open and he was standing there, lit up by the candlelight. He was tall, over six feet, and his shoulders were broad and strong. He wore a long black robe that shimmered in the candlelight. It was all sort of surreal, but it was happening and I knew that I wasn't dreaming. He stood there in the doorway and all I could do was look at him. I realized that he had wings and that he was an angel. His wings though, they were black. They were feathered, but they were black. His skin had an olive complexion. I looked up into his face and what I saw was a handsome man with gentle features. His eyes, they were solid black. There was not a glint of white or any other color there, they were as black as the night. He wasn't smiling but he wasn't frowning either. I took a deep breath. I knew who he was. This was the angel of death.

'You've come for my grandmother, haven't you?' I asked.

He reached forward and touched my shoulder. I felt an instant calmness come over me. All the days of worry and stress just vanished, and I knew that despite how hard this was going to be, it was time, and it would be all right.

I asked again about my grandmother and I saw him slowly shake his head. I closed my eyes as he removed his hand, still feeling the calm wash over me. I thought it was only a moment, but when I opened my eyes, he was gone.

The door was standing open and the wind was blowing in, blowing on the candles, but there was nothing there. No angel, no one.

I closed the door and ran in to check on my grandmother. She was still sound asleep. I planted myself at her bedside until the sun rose, determined to be there in her last minutes. She woke with the morning sun though and sat up in bed, she almost seemed a little better.

I went to go make some food for her and my grandfather. My shock came when I went to wake him up. He had passed away in his sleep."

Lia then stopped trying to hold back her tears. She had been so focused on the illness her grandmother was fighting that she didn't understand who the angel of death had truly come for.

"That's why he shook his head when I asked about my grandmother. It

wasn't her time that night and I didn't understand. He tried to give me some comfort but I didn't realize it."

Lia slowly walked in to her grandmother's bedroom, struggling to find a way to break the news to her. She stood for a moment, her mouth moving but nothing coming out.

"I… he." Lia stammered.

"Oh, I know dear. He passed away peacefully in his sleep. He was determined to go ahead of me so he could be there to welcome me."

Lia was stunned again. Somehow, her grandmother already knew her beloved husband had passed away in the night. She saw the tears flowing from her grandmother's eyes, but there was a smile there too.

"It's all right dear, he didn't suffer and I won't be far behind him now."

Lia spent the next two days catnapping while her grandmother was resting. She usually slept on the sofa in the living room, close to the open door of her grandmother's bedroom.

On the third night, her grandmother stayed up late. They talked about religion and family. Her grandmother made a point of recalling some of the many traditions and folk cures she had taught Lia over the years. Finally, the elderly woman laid down and fell into a deep sleep. Lia stayed by her bed for a time until finally going to the kitchen for a late snack.

"I ate some bread and some cheese then I went into the living room. I had just laid down on the sofa intending to take a nap while my grandmother slept.

Just as I put my head down, my attention was drawn to the front door. It swung slowly open and he was standing there again. I knew right away what it meant. It was her time now. I wanted to get up, to go in there and be by her side but something made me fall into a deep sleep. I believe that it was him, Azrael, the archangel of death. He put me to sleep while he entered to take my grandmother home. I woke up early in the morning. I bolted up at first, but then I just sat there on the sofa for a moment. I listened but I didn't hear anything in the house. I walked slowly to the bedroom but I already knew what I would find. My grandmother had passed away with a little smile on her face. She looked completely peaceful.

I went back out to the living room to make the phone call and it was then that I realized all the candles on the altar had gone out.

My grandparents had died within just a couple of days of each other and I knew that it's the way they wanted things to be."

Lia then sat back taking another drink of her coffee. She seemed better, as though telling the story again was cathartic for her. I had questions to ask, details I was curious about, but they could wait. The power of her story sat with me for a long time after our first meeting.

Lia was confident her grandparents passed in peace and she has no doubt that when her time comes, the tall figure in black will arrive at the door to escort her to the afterlife.

Lia is not alone in her belief that she encountered the angel of death. Indeed, Azrael has a large following, and stories abound about encounters with him. Black wings and black eyes are common themes in his appearances, although like many angelic beings, he is capable of taking many forms.

Lia herself is part of a network of people from around the world who all believe they have encountered the angel of death and that their lives have improved as a result of being in his presence.

While one would expect the appearance of this figure to cause fear and stress, many people report a feeling of calmness and a sense of peace from their experiences with him. They are comforted by the awareness that death is not a frightening figure looming out of the darkness, but a being who can help souls make a gentle transition out of this life and into what lies beyond.

Chapter 19

Changelings

A changeling is the offspring of a troll, elf, or other fairy being that has been switched for a human child. Tales of changelings can be found in a large portion of Western Europe from Ireland and Scotland, to Scandinavia and Spain. The legends are especially strong in countries with fairy (sometimes called fay) or 'wee folk' traditions.

Legends say these supernatural creatures arrive in the night, bringing one of their own offspring and leaving it in place of a human child. The more attractive the human child, the greater the danger of it being stolen by fairies.

Folklore reveals a wide variety of reasons the fay switch their children for human babies. Some traditions claim the wee folk need humans to prevent extensive inbreeding and the destruction of their race. (An idea that has conveyed over into the lore and theories involving the alien grays). Others believe fairy children require the milk of human mothers in order to survive. Still other traditions claim the fairy people want humans to raise as servants, or in more dreaded tales, as sacrifices for evil, demonic gods.

At times, the human child is not replaced with a living being at all. The fairies have the power to enchant a piece of wood called a 'fetch' or 'stock' to resemble the child they take. Such an illusion won't hold long, however, as the fetch usually withers away and the 'child' appears to die.

Changelings appear to be human in most regards so they can't always be spotted right away. Over time, they begin to exhibit strange behavior because of their true, fay nature. Changelings are said to cry or scream excessively. They might have fits of anger, or speak in strange tongues. They will exhibit huge appetites, and can cause people around them to become weak and sick.

According to the lore of changelings, physical changes often give away fay origins. Shifts in hair or eye color, distortions of limbs, or marks and colorations on the skin are all indications a child has been switched and a changeling is present.

There are a variety of folk cures to reveal a changeling, and force the return of the human child. Herbs, potions and talismans can be created to make the child reveal its true nature. Often, the very threat of mistreatment is enough to force the fay to return the human baby and reclaim the changeling lest harm befall it.

In Ireland, fire is the remedy to recover a human child taken by the fay. It's believed that throwing a changeling into a fireplace will cause it to escape up the chimney and then the human child is returned—a brutal remedy that was hopefully not a widespread practice.

In times past, such terrible solutions often led human parents to remain quiet, even if they believed their child had been switched for a fairy. The human parents would raise the changeling as their own son or daughter. Some of these changelings would, over time, forget their true nature and continue to live as a human. Most, however, would eventually leave without warning, wandering into the wild to return to their fay families.

It's likely that a lack of understanding of medical conditions and infant illnesses made a large contribution to the widespread belief in changelings. Conditions such as Down's syndrome, cerebral palsy, and autism would have frightened many people and caused them to think magic was afoot. Especially since there was no understanding of such conditions until the modern era of medicine. Additionally, parents with a child who suddenly became ill, or began to exhibit unusual behavior, desperately tried to find explanations to understand their dilemma. Superstition, and fear of the supernatural, lead to wild theories to explain what would now be recognized as medical conditions. The infamous fairy people made for good scapegoats since they were troublesome in so many other ways.

Fortunately, the church offered salvation if the parents acted quickly enough. Religious leaders claimed that the best defense against the faerie realm was baptism. Coming into the fold of the church would offer protection against the dark forces of the fairy world, and keep demons from harming or taking a child. A child who was baptized was blessed by the power of the church and was protected from any supernatural beings that might try to switch him for one of their own, or for an enchanted object. The church itself let this belief grow as it gave them greater authority, and gained converts of the parents as well as the children.

Modern Changelings

Belief in changelings continued to endure in parts of Europe as late as the 19th century. In 1826 in County Kerry, Ireland, an elderly woman named Ann Roche believed a four-year-old boy was a changeling.

Michael Leahy was unable to walk, stand, or speak. Ann Roche became convinced the boy was 'fairy struck' and that the fay were responsible for his ailments. Roche decided she could drive the fay out of him by using water. She bathed the boy several times in the river Flesk. Her attempts were so vigorous, that on the third time in the water, she drowned the boy. Roche was arrested and stood trial for the child's murder. A jury listened as Ann Roche gave her testimony. She swore she wasn't trying to harm the child at all; she simply wanted to drive the changeling out, and break the fairy's hold on the boy. The jury believed Ann Roche's story and passed a verdict of not guilty.

Bridget Cleary

Another case occurred in 1895 in Ireland, and involved a twenty-six-year-old woman named Bridget Cleary. Bridget was killed by a group of people that included her husband, Michael, and her cousins, all of whom believed she was a changeling.

The story of Bridget's tragic death began on a cold day in March 1895, when Bridget went to visit neighbors near a place called Kylenagranagh Hill. The spot was notorious for being a haunt of the fairies. Jack Dunne, the man who lived there, was widely regarded as a man connected to the fay. Rumors claimed the location was connected to powerful, dark fairy magic, and most people avoided it as much as possible. Bridget was not concerned with such stories however.

Finding the Dunne's were not at home, Bridget returned to her house. She had caught a chill during her walk and sat by the fire trying to get warm. By the next day, the cold in her bones was accompanied by a severe headache. In the following days, Bridget's condition worsened, and she developed pneumonia.

Family members began to talk about where Bridget had been, and what exactly might be affecting her. They all knew she had been on Kylenagranagh Hill, and they speculated about what may have happened on that cold day. When Jack Dunne himself visited Bridget, he left the room whispering that the woman he had just seen in the bed was not Bridget Cleary.

People began to talk about the possibility that Bridget had been abducted by the fay and replaced with a stock. Bridget's husband, Michael, began to speak openly about his wife's transformation. He claimed she was a fay creature and that everyone was in danger of her evil powers.

Michael visited a man named Denis Ganey in Kyleatlea. Ganey was highly regarded as a 'fairy doctor' and Michael hoped he would offer a solution for his wife's affliction. The two talked for some time, and when Michael left Ganey's house, he carried home a potion to help with the situation.

As events began to unfold, the story became even stranger. Michael's behavior became violent and irrational. He and several of Bridget's cousins held her down and forced her to take the medicine sent by Ganey. They later held her over a fire in a further attempt to drive the fay out and bring back the real Bridget. They ignored her screams of pain.

By March 15th, Michael Cleary had lost all sense of reason. That evening, he soaked his wife in paraffin and set her on fire. Michael Clearly believed that by burning the body, his real wife would return to him riding on a white horse. Other family members did nothing to stop the murder.

Soon, the police were involved in a search for the missing woman. Cleary continued to insist his wife had left and he didn't know where she was. Michael Cleary and several others were eventually arrested and put on trial for murder in July 1895.

Michael Cleary was sentenced to twenty years on charges of manslaughter while in a disturbed state. Several other people, including Bridget's cousins, received time for their part in forcing Bridget to take 'medicine' that was actually poisonous to humans.

Throughout his trial, Michael Cleary continued to insist the fay had abducted his wife, and he only wanted to help her return. He insisted he needed to wait for her on a nearby hill, where she would return to him now that the 'changeling' had been burned.

The sad case of Bridget Cleary is an example of what can happen when people are overwhelmed by the fear of things they don't understand. The idea of fairy abductions has long had strong roots across much of Europe. Even in fairly modern times, in some rural areas, normal, working class people have quickly become irrational when they believe loved ones have been switched for something sinister and unknown.

Tales of changelings are still popular in modern storytelling. Books, television and movies have all used the enduring legend as a plot device. Some researchers also find numerous correlations between fairy abductions and modern accounts of UFO abductees.

Perhaps there really is something out there, waiting for an opportunity to steal us away and replace us with an enchanted fetch.

Chapter 20

Succubus

They come in the night. Mostly to those who sleep alone. To men, they appear as a beautiful woman, to women, they appear as a handsome man. They are dream lovers, fantasies that straddle the edge of sleep and waking consciousness, and they are much more. They are energy draining, vampiric entities, out to steal as much energy and vitality as they can from those they consider their prey.

They are demonic creatures known as the succubus.

The term 'succubus' is derived from a Latin word meaning 'to lie under.' The male version of the entity is referred to as an 'incubus' from a Latin term meaning 'to lie upon.' Succubi and Incubi are the plural terms for these entities.

Historical Succubi

During the infamous European witch-hunts, succubi and incubi were common topics during trials of witches. The dreadful beings were thought to be agents of the devil that attempted to catch people off guard while they were sleeping. The succubus/incubus would offer sexual pleasure and sometimes promises of power or immortality.

It was thought women were more vulnerable to such demonic influence, so cases involving incubi were more common.

Demonologists of the period were still hung up on the idea Eve was to blame for original sin and the expulsion from Eden, hence women were more likely to fall into league with the devil and engage in relations with lovers from the demonic realms.

According to the text used by the Inquisitors, the *'Malleus Maleficarum'* or, the 'Hammer of the Witches,' women who practiced witchcraft would willingly engage in relations with incubi, using the sexual act to further their connection to Satan.

Inquisitors believed if a succubus attacked a man, the man was probably not to blame and could be forgiven. Taking the form of a beautiful woman, the succubus would cause a man to have erotic dreams that lead to nocturnal emissions, thus the creature could steal his creative energy. The theft of life force and energy was one of the main goals of the succubus/incubus.

It was also believed a succubus could become pregnant by a human and bear a demon child. These hybrid children would become especially powerful in the demonic realms as they carried the energy of earth and hell in the same body. The combination would allow the entity to travel freely between the two realms.

According to accounts, relations with these creatures were far from a pleasant experience. When engaging with a succubus, the act itself was purported to be painful and akin to penetrating a cavern of ice. Incubi often harmed the women they seduced because of their misshapen forms and violent behavior. The succubus and incubus reveled in creating pain and doing harm to their human lovers, all while draining their victims of strength and life force.

It was believed a succubus would continue to return to the same victim each night until she had drained him completely of his life energy. A man who fell victim to such a creature would feel tired and sickly the next day. If left unchecked, a rapid decline in health would result, followed eventually by death. This process could take several nights depending on the constitution of the victim. For obvious reasons, those with a strong mind and body were especially attractive to demonic lovers.

The succubus was usually invisible to everyone except her victim. With the ability to take any form, the creature would often manifest in the image of the victim's innermost desire. While they were said to be most attracted to single men, no one was considered safe from their allure.

Common defenses against these demonic energy thieves included holy water, reciting the Ave Maria, making the sign of the cross, and saying the Lord's Prayer. If a succubus made numerous visits to a victim, a priest was required to break the connection and banish the demon for good.

The incubus was more inclined to torment his victims, forcing them to commit greater and greater sins with each visit. The incubus would whisper instructions into the ear of a woman, creating paranoia, fear, and jealousy. The incubus was also an energy-draining creature, but he took his greatest pleasure in degrading and perverting the women he targeted.

Both the male incubus, and the female succubus, could be summoned by those who practiced the black arts.

Queen of the Succubi

Hebrew tradition teaches that Adam's first wife, Lilith was also the first succubus. Lilith is a major figure in Hebrew myth and demonology, and she is feared even today in some areas of the world.

According to ancient Jewish texts, Lilith was outraged at the idea of submitting to her husband, Adam, and demanded she be treated as his equal. When she was refused this request, she fled the Garden of Eden and went to the wastelands of the deserts near the Red Sea. There, she became the bride of the fallen angel Samael, or, Lucifer, the devil himself by some accounts.

Lilith is connected to the Moon. After being cast out of Eden, her power became stronger at night, especially during full moons. Her rage was such that, each night, she would travel out across the world, seek men in their sleep, and seduce them. In this way, she bore an infinite number of demon children. Over time, her demonic offspring spread far and wide across the globe.

It is said Lilith lurks beneath doorways and in wells, waiting for lone men she can seduce. The Hebrews called her the 'demon of screeching,' and she has been closely linked with wild animals, and specifically, the screech owl, the form of which she is able to assume.

Lilith is first mentioned as early as 700 B.C.E. and her origin probably began with the Babylonians or the Sumerians. She appears in various forms in cultures and mythologies around the world. During the medieval period in Europe, Lilith was thought to be the wife, or concubine of Satan and was sometimes called the queen of witches.

Numerous magical amulets were made to protect pregnant women and infant children from the power of Lilith. She was reputed to be especially fond of attacking young children in their sleep, causing illness or death.

Men were not safe from Lilith's wrath either. After seducing them, she would often lure them to their deaths—her way of seeking vengeance for being asked to submit to a man.

Chapter 21

Spirits Of The Dreaming

Tribal cultures around the world believe there is more to existence than the mere physical realm. Shamanic practitioners utilize a wide variety of techniques to access other dimensions of reality. Their altered states of consciousness include trance work, shamanic dreaming and journeys, and vision quests. Through entering these altered states, the shaman can work with spiritual guides, heal the inner self, and obtain vital information to assist others.

For practitioners who use these techniques, there are many levels of the dreaming state. 'Upper' and 'lower' worlds exist, and are populated with beings that can offer either assistance or destruction. Learning to navigate these other levels of reality takes time, training, and patience. It's not a path to be taken lightly, and those who follow such traditions are very careful about who they let participate.

Shamanic Dreamers

Jose is a practitioner of shamanic traditions from Central America. He has traveled extensively, and worked with a wide variety of native teachers. Jose has a vast range of knowledge in the religio-magical traditions of his part of the world. He is an expert in the healing arts utilizing herbs and other treatments to remove sickness from the mind, body, and spirit. Whether the patient is afflicted by a curse, or a stomachache, Jose usually has a solution to offer.

I spoke with Jose at length about some of the personal experiences he's had doing work in altered states of consciousness.

For Jose, the 'dreaming' is a trance induced state he enters at will. The experiences are lucid and he returns with very clear memories of his time in the altered state. To onlookers, if they didn't know better, it would look as if Jose was simply taking a siesta but, in reality, he would be traveling through a vast world of spiritual beings.

Often, Jose enters a trance state to consult with his guides prior to doing healing work on others. He receives prophetic information while in trance, and gains insight as to how he can best help his client.

Jose says the dream world is filled with spirits of all degrees of good and evil. In a series of visits to these realms, Jose has fought an evil entity with dark eyes that can shape shift. He said of the spirit:

"I have met this being three different times and I had to conquer it each time so that it would not win and take my spirit or energy. It wants my power and it wants my life. It is already powerful and it is very deceptive."

Jose is in his late fifties. He has the rugged appearance of someone who has spent most of their life outdoors, but he has the mind and energy of a much younger man. He traveled most of South and Central America during his youth to pursue what he termed his "calling to be a healer." He set out to explore native spiritual traditions and culture and found much more than he bargained for. He dedicated years of study to becoming a healer and shaman.

Jose smoked a long pipe with a strange concoction of herbs while we sat and talked. We were sparsely covered under the ramshackle roof of a porch that barely kept the pouring rain from reaching us. He offered me a smoke, telling me it's good for the lungs, but I passed on the offer, unsure exactly what was mixed in the pile of herbs. Jose shrugged and continued his story.

"The first time, I was a young man in my twenties and the being came to me in the form of a beautiful woman. At first, I could only see the shape, the body of a nice shaped young woman. She had long flowing hair and the scent of flowers. I have to tell you, she was compelling. Just the thing for a young man.

She was beckoning me to come closer to her and I started to go. Then I stopped, remembering my teacher's words about staying on path. In my vision, the path was literal and it was below my feet. I think I was the only one who could see it, how it twisted and turned into the distance. I could feel it too. It had a soft vibration under my feet.

I kept looking at that woman, thinking how good she looked and how I wanted to touch her. I took a step off that path and right away, I felt like something was wrong. Then she started calling to me, calling me by my name. I started to think maybe this was someone I knew because we can meet fellow dreamers in these states. Maybe this was a woman that I was supposed to go to, to be with. I hadn't met my wife yet so maybe this was her. She kept right on calling to me, motioning for me to come to her with both of her arms open.

I asked her to tell me her name but she didn't answer me. I started to step back so that I was all the way on my path and then she came forward some. I still couldn't see all the details of her face, but I could see more of her body now, she hardly had any clothes on and it was very tempting to go to her. There was a sound in her voice that didn't feel right to me then. I knew that something was wrong and that I shouldn't move from my path. I was protected there and I intended to stay right on it. I even started to move on the path.

I think she got angry with me then. She became loud, telling me I had to come to her now and we had to be together because it was the plan of the spirits. I raised my hand, I was carrying a small lamp, and I wanted to shine the light on her. When the light hit her face, she smiled at me and put her finger to her lips. She was trying to distract me, to keep me from looking up at her eyes, but I had already seen them, they were black as the night and I knew then that she was nothing but an evil spirit, trying to change the direction of my life. The eyes are windows to the true spirit, what you see there will reveal what is in the heart of the person. That is why she couldn't hide what she was from me.

She got angry when I turned and she screamed at me. It sounded like a bird, like the screech of some large bird, maybe a condor or vulture. I looked back at her and I saw those eyes again, black and without a soul. Her mouth was open making that sound and I saw that her teeth were sharp."

Jose says he was in a trance to find help from his guides about his personal direction, and how he should move forward with his training:

"I was at a turning point then. I wanted to seek out a teacher that I had heard about, but people were telling me not to go. I went into the dream world to speak with my guides, to get direction as to what to do next. I think because I was at a critical point, that is why that being came and tried to distract me."

Jose believes he encountered the same entity on two other occasions in his life. Both times the entity was in a different form, but Jose said he recognized the creature anyway:

"The second time was years later. I was working on healing someone, a mother of three who was very ill. That entity came and tried to tell me I was doing something wrong, that I was hurting the woman and that she was going to die anyway. This time, the being was in the form of my father who had died when I was young.

This time I was even closer to it. I thought at first the eyes were black but then it looked as if there were just no eyes there at all, just empty holes. When I didn't listen to it, the being got very angry just like the first time. It started screaming and it was hard to bear the sound. I got away from it as quickly as I could."

Jose said the third encounter with the strange spirit was the most difficult one of all. He hesitated for a long moment, taking a puff from his pipe. He reached into a cooler and extracted two beers that were barely cold. I opened them both and handed him one. He took a long drink then looked out at the rain awhile before continuing his story:

"That last time, it was the hardest of all the encounters. I was much older and I had learned many things about doing this work. But the spirit came in the form of a child, a child that said she needed help and that only I could save her. I could not bear the thought to leave a child behind that needed me. That child tried many things to trick me; she cried, and tried to catch me off my guard. Many things happened in that vision. I don't want to talk about them all. It was the closest that thing, that evil being, has come to taking me, to taking my spirit. I was lucky to see clearly before it was too late, to see that it was the same being without a soul that was trying to steal my power."

Jose sat back, shaking his head in a positive gesture of his success in the dreamtime. He took another long puff on the pipe he held and exhaled the smoke slowly. He watched as the smoke rose into the sky, lost for a moment in his thoughts:

"These beings, they can't change everything about their appearance. They can change their shape, their size, but the eyes are the mirrors of the soul and those they cannot change no matter what. If we are smart and pay attention, this is how we can know them, this is how we can defeat them. The only power they have over us is the power we give them by choice or by mistake."

Jose's teachings tell him these creatures of the dreaming are evil spirits, sent to tempt or trick a shaman into giving away his power. Had he fallen for one of these lures, Jose believes not only would he have lost his ability to heal, but he himself would have fallen very ill or worse.

"I knew someone, a man who fell for the tricks of one of these beings. He was a good man and he had some training in the ways of a healer. But then he met one of these dark beings in his dreamtime and it changed him. Afterwards, he didn't have his vision anymore (referring to his psychic vision). *Then he became very sick, no one could help him, no one knew what it was that afflicted him, but it ate him up inside. He was in a lot of pain. After almost one year of that, he died in his sleep. I believe the evil came back and claimed the rest of his spirit."*

I asked Jose if he thought these evil spirits could take form in the physical world, and if he thought it could explain some of the encounters people have with strange creatures that often vanish into nothingness:

"Yes, I think so, yes. If they steal enough energy from people, I believe that they can use it to take physical form. They come into our world and they create even more disturbances and dark acts. Their abilities are ancient, and they spend all of their time trying to steal power from people so they can use it for more evil. They want life force. They know how to take it, and they know how to use it in many ways. If they come into our physical world, I believe they will thrive and they will be much harder to fight against."

Jose believes he will encounter the beings in the dream world again. For him, they appear during critical times in his life, when he is vulnerable, or when he reaches turning points in his training:

"It is important to stay aware. If you ever see such beings, look at them closely, they cannot hide their true nature. But beware; you never know what form such evil will take when next it comes."

Those like Jose, who choose to work with the power of the dreamtime, and delve into trance states, find a world of knowledge few people ever access. It's also a world filled with dangers to the mind, body, and spirit.

Jose spoke in simple terms about his work, his beliefs, and about his path as a healer. It may be easy for the average person to dismiss such notions as primitive or uneducated, but the reality is, Jose and others like him, are effective healers and important members of their communities. They often fill multiple roles in their villages, serving as healers, therapists, and priests. Whether you interpret such things as mystical, or as another aspect of the human mind, the fact is, for these practitioners, reality is much more than what most people perceive it to be.

While the road of the shaman is not an easy one, it's a path that offers techniques of empowerment and access to greater levels of human consciousness. If creatures from the dream world, or from some other level of existence, have found their way into our physical, waking world, Shaman such as Jose may be the ones who can offer us keys to overcome them and put an end to their dark plans.

Chapter 22

Final Thoughts

The black eyed children are now solidly rooted in the realm of the paranormal. There's no doubt reports will continue to come in and people will continue to encounter these odd children.

With the continued interest in all things paranormal, it's likely further study will be done, and more accounts collected. Perhaps the BEKs will 'slip up' and be caught on camera, but will it matter? The fear these beings create won't translate to a photo, and critics will simply say it's a boy with contacts. What matters most, is the effect these beings have on the people who encounter them.

I have interviewed countless people over the years, and I have listened to endless tales of encounters with black eyed beings. And yet, at the end of the day, there are many stories that cannot be told.

A large percentage of witnesses simply don't want their stories presented in any form, anonymous or otherwise. They shared their accounts with me because I was willing to listen and could confirm they were not alone in their experience. I hope that I gave them a little more understanding, and maybe some comfort, in dealing with what they had experienced. But for many, to have their stories put out to the world was just too much to ask. Those who feel this way only want to forget their experience and move forward with their lives.

Like the ones presented in this book, their stories vary. Some are brief encounters; others are long, detailed accounts. Like the stories you've read here, they all share similar qualities and there is something unnerving about each and every one of them.

The black eyed kids want something. What exactly they want is not clear. What is clear, is, they are determined to continue pressing into people's lives when least expected. The more the mystery of the BEKs is examined, the deeper it seems to go. Is there indeed some greater, sinister agenda behind these children? While some people think they are aliens or ghosts, others believe they are an old devil in a new guise. Perhaps we shall never discover what the black eyed children truly are, or what they represent, but by all appearances, they are here to stay.

The reports are oddly compelling. People are both disturbed and intrigued by accounts of the BEKs. While some people claim they would actually like to see one of these beings, I'm most often asked if there is anything one can do to avoid meeting the black eyed children. Not knowing their origins, this is an impossible question to answer. All that remains is to pay attention and be aware.

There's just one more thing.

If at the end of a long day, just as you are getting comfortable, you hear a gentle rap on the door, it may be safer to simply not answer.

Brian Bethel
20 Years Later

When I first began to delve into accounts of the black eyed children, at the top of my agenda was attempting to contact the people behind some of the more intriguing accounts published online. Number one on that list was, of course, Brian Bethel.

Bethel's encounter is discussed earlier in this book and, as I've stated, it's the one responsible for kicking off the modern wave of BEK reports. I had tried to contact Brian previously, back in the late nineties specifically, not too long after his original report started circulating widely on the world wide web. I never heard back from him then, and years later, when I was writing the book you now hold, I tried to reach him again. Yet again, I received no response. The first time, I expect he was simply overwhelmed from receiving countless emails about the incident. The second time, I would later learn, was due to his self-imposed seclusion, again, the result of being overwhelmed by endless questions about the infamous children.

Investigators meet with disappointment all the time, and one must merely press on, gathering facts and finding other paths to the required information necessary to reach the end result. Unfortunately, I had to publish the first edition of the book without personally interviewing Brian or getting more direct information from him. I found as much about his original postings and account as I could and included the story since it was so critical.

It was well after the book was published that Brian and I finally

221

got in touch with each other, though as of this publication, we have yet to meet in person. Long distance impressions, such as they are, yet I've found Brian to be intelligent, well read, and a bit on the low-key side. It's clear after the excitement of the "viral" story about the BEKs, Brian found himself in the middle of something he never expected. Eventually, it became too much and he had to retreat for a time.

It's hard to believe it's now been twenty years since Bethel had his encounter, an inadvertently perfect time to release this revised edition of my study of the phenomena of the BEKs.

I'm happy to include the dialogue below from Brian as he reflects on his experience, and its aftermath, twenty years after the event.

Brian Bethel & The Black Eyed Kids

When Brian posted his account, he certainly didn't expect such a rapid response. He was simply looking for answers and, hopefully, some insight as to what he had seen. The exposure that resulted from the posting of his encounter took him by surprise:

"This was in the early days of the Internet, at least comparatively. So, in some respects, the story went "viral" before we even had such terminology. I really didn't understand what was happening or why. I was at first impressed by the response, then overwhelmed. The first few trickles of inquiry turned into a vast flood over time.

I still cannot believe that something I wrote that wasn't really intended to be widely shared has found such legs. It's been both wonderful and frustrating, for reasons I'll explain later on.

I do wish that the BEK acronym hadn't caught on. It's an easy shorthand, to be sure, but I think it somewhat limits what we can talk about in regard to the phenomenon. Not all sightings are of children, so the "kids" part of the acronym comes from me being a bit flip in my initial story. I've often wished I'd used the terms "beings" or something similar instead. But, like it or not, BEK is here to stay, I suppose."

When asked if he'd had contact with other witnesses who met the same children he encountered, Bethel said that while he hasn't personally met any, he does believe the kids he ran into could have been responsible for other incidents:

"I can honestly say no, though I will qualify that statement in a bit. A gentleman recently told me of what I regard as a credible sighting not far away from Abilene, where I still live. What he saw was a young boy and a young girl.

Reports often have the children wearing hoodies, like in my original story, but you also hear reports of them wearing outdated clothing. In many cases, they're dressed in current fashion or otherwise innocuous in appearance. Descriptions vary, and often all one gets from witnesses would be the gender and approximate age.

Is it possible that some of the same children have been involved in other encounters? Perhaps. But I've read nothing to suggest to me that others have encountered exactly the same two children I have. I'll admit it has to be within the realm of possibility—and even probability. There seems to be some disagreement on if and how these entities "age." If they age like humans, then those "kids" should be in at least their latter 20s by now. If they don't, then who knows? Some people believe they can alter their appearance, at least somewhat. I will say if I could prove someone had seen the exact same children, especially years later, I would consider that vastly significant."

Like most other people who have had run ins with the BEK, Bethel suffered his share of after-effects. He was plagued with lack of sleep, paranoia, and other symptoms long after the encounter. In fact, he reports the traumatic effects still linger:

"For the first few weeks after, my sleep was greatly disturbed. I have trouble sleeping anyway, and I fell into full insomnia after the encounter. I didn't want to sleep—I felt unsafe doing so. I kept having this fantasy of them appearing at the foot of my bed, or waiting outside my door for me when I went outside. It was a rough few weeks, I'll say, and the effects linger to this day. The use of black eyes to symbolize evil has become a common trope in horror films and other media, and I will tell you that every time I see such an image, especially if I'm not expecting it, I flash back briefly to those terrible, agonizing moments in my car. I legitimately did not know if I was going to die or not. I have never been so terrified.

There was a pervading sense of being watched that I associate with the first few months after my encounter, and that feeling still returns from time to time when I talk about that experience. In interviews I've given, equipment has tended to malfunction or act strangely, and I've noted odd electrical phenomena on my own when I've been discussing the event. I'll add that for a period of time afterward, my luck turned remarkably bad. It righted itself a few months later, but the number of odd things that transpired seemed far greater than chance would allow.

223

The phenomenon occurs to a lesser degree it seems, when we talk about it even now. During my television interview, for example, our beloved cat of many, many years suddenly disappeared without explanation, and my partner and I became ill. The timing was again uncanny, and television producers appear to have little sympathy for those desperately trying to find a lost pet when it conflicts with their schedules. Our cat's name was Beba, and Judie still jokes, "the BEKs took my Beba away." Except neither one of us really regards it as a joke.

At the time of my encounter, I was going through some great spiritual and mental changes, things happening internally that still color my life and outlook. I believe in part what attracted them to me was those internal changes. While I don't plan to go entirely into what was going on, I actually remain grateful for the experience because it taught me to trust my intuition, a confirmation that these internal alterations needed to flourish."

It's interesting to note Brian never intended for his encounter to be released to a wide audience. The story got out when someone from an online community released the account and other people began to share it. But why did Brian post the account to begin with? His simple answer, "catharsis." Bethel has always been a writer, so his natural outlet for trying to deal with the experience was through writing:

"As I said, I have never been so frightened in my life. I am a writer by trade, but I'm one of those people who would write even if there wasn't a paycheck involved. It's just in you. I often deal with things by writing them down, an act I find comforting by itself. I wrote my story to deal with the fear and to create a record, and I initially shared that record with a small number of people on a private email mailing list who I felt would be sympathetic. Similarly, I posted the story to a ghost story/paranormal community on Usenet that had long been supportive. From there, it leaked out slowly and in time became what it is now. It was a story meant for relatively few that has suddenly become the "property" of the very many. Information wants to be free, so I understand how and why it has proliferated.

I stand by my original account, and I will continue to do so. I do admittedly worry that there is now a "template" for a BEK story, as there is for alien abduction stories. Through popular culture and later parody, everyone has an archetypal idea of what an alien abduction is like and entails. (Please note, I'm not advocating the objective reality of such experiences, simply noting that there is a popularly-accepted form and format.)

There is now a BEK "template" promulgated through websites, forums and discussions, and I worry that muddies the waters for serious researchers. It's easy now to write something quasi-convincing based on that model—kids knock on a car window or door, ask to come in, door opener detects something is wrong, terrible revelation, rinse and repeat.

I judge each story shared with me on its own merits, but I apply greater skepticism to anything that adheres too slavishly to the basic formula. I look and listen for little variations and details that add more verisimilitude. If it's just a carbon copy of what I've heard or seen, I tend to dismiss it or at least give it less credence.

That said, I have heard many, many stories I'm convinced are true. In the aforementioned case where the gentleman saw something fairly near to Abilene, he was standing right in front of me telling his story. I saw goosebumps rise on arms, his voice became broken with fear. He wasn't faking, and while I'm certain a huge number of alleged BEK sightings are bunk, I'm also convinced there are many others that are frighteningly real."

Despite the passage of time, Bethel feels no closer to having an answer for what he experienced, nor an answer to what the black eyed children are. Like others who have researched and investigated the accounts, and like those who have experienced the BEKs personally, he remains disturbed and puzzled:

"The fundamental question: What are they? Is the one that vexes me most. In the time I've been discussing these entities, I've heard them described by others as vampires, alien-human hybrids, dark faeries, demons, extra-dimensional beings—the list is vast. I had one good friend suggest they are servants of a dark goddess that stretches back to ancient Sumeria. The preacher's wife at the church I attended when I was a kid told me a few years ago her study group had discussed them and dubbed them children of the Nephilim, the fallen angels from the Book of Genesis. Of course, I've had plenty of people insist they were figments of my own imagination.

The one thing I didn't do, and I will mention this here, is make them up. You'll find nothing gets me angrier than reading on some website or another that I "created" the BEKs. Good, solid research by folks like David Weatherly and others proves that I didn't. There are stories that predate mine, and that's something of a comfort, even if the implication of such longevity isn't all that comforting."

As Bethel states, the fundamental question remains: What are they? It's something Brian has thought about often over the years since his encounter. Today, when he's asked this primary question, and he's asked it all the time, his answer is simple:

"I don't know.

That answer may frustrate people who want an end point to all of this discussion, but I would be lying if I said I could give any other. I tend toward something we would term demonic, but these descriptions tend to fail pretty quickly.

What I do know about them is they are predators, and we are the food. I don't think they eat us in any literal sense, but they do want something from us. These are beings that have no light within them, soulless and eternally hungry. What their ultimate aim is I find difficult to divine, but I know they mean their victims irreparable harm. Perhaps they make more of their kind this way, or perhaps they just steal the light within us to better perfect their guises. Maybe they do just want to kill, but I tend to think the design is far more complex than that. This is all simply intuition, but I've heard similar things from others.

Until you've been on the receiving end of those terrible, dark eyes, filled with hate and torn from the very depths of night and time, I'm not sure you can understand. The people I've spoken with who have truly seen them understand completely.

I wish I had better answers. I'm sorry."

From his story going viral, to, at times, being credited for the entire phenomenon, to wrestling with how to resolve his place in the study of the topic, where does Brian find himself today in terms of his place in the modern history of BEK accounts?

"I've gone through several phases when it comes to the BEK story. At first, I was eager to share information and theories with any and all comers — and there have at this point been literally hundreds of people who have contacted me through the years. Subsequently, I went through a period when I didn't want to talk about it at all. In retrospect, I would change that, but I felt like I was genuinely answering the same half-dozen questions over and over again.

I created a FAQ file, which I submitted to my friend Lisa Krause's website, Ghosts.org, the sort of unofficial "home" of my writings dealing with paranormal events. I let that stand as my standard answer for quite a while. That period of absence was when things really took off, and I regret not being present, so to speak, for that period. I would have in retrospect like to have been more involved when new encounters were posted. At the same time, there was a lot of misinformation that seemed to start circulating at the time about both my own experience and the entities themselves. I most sincerely regret not getting back to any number of people in that period who asked me for help, interviews or further information. There was more than a bit of frustration expressed at my silence, and I would go back and change things if I could.

A few years ago, at the prompting of my partner, I stepped out of my shell and started communicating with folks again. In this new period, I've collected a remarkable number of personal anecdotes, some truly chilling, and have had an opportunity to tell my story online and on television.

I continue to hear from many people willing to share stories and theories. I welcome those communications. I've been a bit frustrated in some cases by those who haven't contacted me—it would have been nice, for example, for "Fortean Times" to try to get in touch before they did their recent article (thought I'll admit it was both well-researched and fair). It's a bit odd to listen in on Coast to Coast or read your name on forum after forum and see or hear what people are saying about you—without you having a chance to weigh in. I've started doing that more openly when opportunities present, but the amount of information out there is simply overwhelming, and I can't hope to reply to everything. The amount of discussion is both fascinating and frustrating.

There are times when I wish the whole thing hadn't happened. There are times I'm intensely grateful that it has. I've met many wonderful and insightful people, most virtually, through this encounter. While I'd had strange experiences before, this experience ripped open the possibility of a supernatural world that cannot be denied. It offers somewhat less comfort than a staid reality where such things cannot exist, but it has also opened up worlds of wonder and insight. I've made not a dime from this incident, and in fact, it's exactly the sort of thing a professional journalist normally wouldn't talk openly about. It's not hurt my credibility, as I hope the fruits of my career will attest, but it often does make for some interesting conversations after my formal interviews with open-minded folks are over."

Although Bethel can't answer the burning question of what the BEK actually are, he does have some additional thoughts on their nature:

"Reality, with a capital R, is far more strange and varied than many interpretations would allow. There are things out there that are wondrous and strange, and there are things out there that mean us harm.

The BEKs, no matter what their origins, are a predator species. They have powers of suggestion and deception that can lead you into a false sense of comfort, one reason I think these beings consciously choose the form of children. They are filled with hatred. They have no soul-light within them.

227

But they are not perfect, they are not insurmountable. A person who is observant, who is careful, who trusts their gut feelings can fetter them out. They have strange sets of rules, including the bizarre affectation of requiring permission to enter a place or personal vehicle. Why is this the case? I don't know, but it's your greatest leverage against them. They cannot invade your space, and thus harm you, unless you allow them permission.

What they might be fully capable of if encountered out and about is still largely unknown, though people have seen them in public places and been approached similarly. If you keep your wits about you, judging from such stories, you can still emerge unharmed but perhaps shaken.

They are dangerous entities, to be sure, but we have something they don't, something they desperately want. I believe it is the light within us, the human soul, that they crave. Whether they wish to corrupt it or consume it, I don't know. But it is that very thing they desire that gives us the edge over them. It is something they apparently can't just take. Permission has to be given, and in that is our strength.

It's good advice in general, but beware who you allow into your life and don't open doors for just anyone. Be discerning. Be aware. And most important, be safe."

I've encouraged Brian to write a book about the black eyed kids. Between his personal encounter and its significance, his reflections on the topic, and the number of people that have contacted him over the years to report their own experiences, I'm sure he could add something to the study of this unusual topic. Whether he decides to or not, I'm grateful for his above contribution to this updated edition of the Black Eyed Children. In some ways, it has brought things full circle. Of course, as with much of the paranormal field, while the information is fascinating, it still leaves us with more questions than answers.

Bibliography

Abrams, Jeremiah & Zweig, Connie. Meeting the Shadow: The Hidden Power of the Dark Side of Human Nature (A New Consciousness Reader). New York, NY: Tarcher Publishing, 1991.

Addiss, Steven. Japanese Ghosts and Demons: Art of the Supernatural. New York, NY: George Braziller Inc., 2001.

Ashcroft-Nowicki, Dolores. & Brennan, J. H. Magical Use of Thought Forms: A Proven System of Mental and Spiritual Empowerment. Woodbury, MN: Llewellyn Worldwide Publishing, 2001.

Barker, Gray. Men In Black The Secret Terror. Seattle, WA: Metadisc Books, 2011.

Barker, Gray. They Knew Too Much About Flying Saucers. New York, NY: University Books, 1956.

Bender, Albert K. Flying Saucers and the Three Men. Clarksburg, WV: Saucerian Books, 1962

Bender, Albert K. Space Review: Complete File of the Publication Issued by the International Flying Saucer Bureau, Bridgeport, CT, from October 1952 through October 1953, Inclusive. Clarksburg, WV: Saucerian Books, 1962.

Besant, Annie & Leadbeater, C.W. Thought Forms. Theosophical Press, 1901.

Birnes, William J. The Everything UFO Book. Avon, MA: Adams Media, 2012.

Brennan, J. H. Occult Tibet: Secret Practices of Himalayan Magic. Woodbury, MN: Llewellyn Worldwide Publishing, 2002.

Briggs, Katharine. An Encyclopedia of Fairies, Hobgoblins, Brownies, Boogies and Other Supernatural Creatures. New York, NY: Pantheon Books, 1976.

Brunvand, Jan Harold. The Choking Doberman. New York, NY: W.W. Norton & Company, 1981.

Brunvand, Jan Harold. The Encyclopedia of Urban Legends. New York, NY: W.W. Norton & Company, 2002.

Bullard, Thomas E. UFO Abductions: The Measure of a Mystery Volumes 1 & 2. Mount Rainier, MD: Fund for UFO Research, 1987.

Burton, Richard Francis. The Book of the Thousand Nights and One Night. New York, NY: Assouline Press, 2006.

Cheung, Theresa. The Element Encyclopedia of Vampires: An A-Z of the Undead. New York, NY: Element Books/Harper, 2009.

Clark, Jerome. The UFO Encyclopedia Vols 1 & 2. Second Edition. Detroit, MI: Omnigraphics, Inc. 1998.

Curran, Bob Dr. Dark Fairies. Franklin Lakes, NJ: Career Press, 2010.

Curran, Bob Dr. Vampires. Franklin Lakes, NJ: Career Press, 2005.

David-Neel, Alexandra. Magic and Mystery in Tibet. Mineola, NY: Dover Publications, 1971.

Davidson, Gustav. A Dictionary of Angels, Including the Fallen Angels. New York, NY: Free Press Publishing, 1994.

Deel, Kenneth. The Catholic Demonologist Handbook, Underground Edition. Swords of Saint Michael Press, 2009.

DiStasi, Lawrence. Mal Occhio (Evil Eye) The Underside of Vision. New York, NY: North Point Press, 1981.

Dundes, Alan. The Evil Eye: A Folklore Casebook. New York, NY: Garland Publishing, Inc., 1981.

Elworthy, Frederick Thomas. The Evil Eye: The Origins and Practices of Superstition. John Murray, London, England, 1895.

Freud, Sigmund & Gay, Peter. The Freud Reader. New York, NY: W.W. Norton & Company, 1995.

Friedman, Stanton & Marden, Kathleen. Captured! The Betty and Barney Hill UFO Experience: The True Story of the World's First Documented Alien Abduction. Pompton Plains, NJ: New Page Books, 2007.

Fuller, John G. The Interrupted Journey: Two Lost Hours Aboard A Flying Saucer. New York, NY: Dial Press, 1966.

Glassie, Henry & Kass, Francine. Irish Folktales (Pantheon Fairy Tale & Folklore Library) New York, NY: Pantheon Books, 1997.

Gold, Peter. Navajo and Tibetan Sacred Wisdom: The Circle of the Spirit. Rochester, VT: Inner Traditions Press, 1994.

Gregory, Richard L. The Oxford Companion to the Mind. New York, NY: Oxford University Press, 1987.

Guiley, Rosemary Ellen. Encyclopedia of Demons & Demonology. New York, NY: Checkmark Books, 2009.

Guiley, Rosemary Ellen. The Djinn Connection: The Hidden Links Between Djinn, Shadow People, ETs, Nephilim, Archons, Reptilians and Other Entities. CT: New Edition, Visionary Living Inc, 2017.

Hambly, Wilfrid Dyson. The History of Tattooing. Mineola, NY: Dover Publications, 2009.

Hanauer, J.E. Folklore of the Holy Land: Moslem, Christian and Jewish (1901). Ithaca, NY: Cornell University Press, 2009.

Hyde, Lewis. Trickster Makes This World: Mischief, Myth and Art. New York, NY: Farrar, Straus & Giroux, 2010.

Jacobs, David M. Secret Life: Firsthand Accounts of UFO Abductions. New York, NY: Simon and Shuster, 1992.

Johnson, Robert A. Owning Your Own Shadow: Understanding the Dark Side of the Psyche. San Francisco, CA: Harper Publishing, 1993.

Jung, C. G. The Archetypes and the Collective Unconscious. Princeton, NJ: Princeton University Press, 1981.

Jung, C. G. <u>Man and His Symbols.</u> London, 1978.

Jung, C. G. <u>Psychology of the Unconscious.</u> London, 1944.

Keel, John A. <u>The Mothman Prophecies.</u> New York, NY: Saturday Review Press/E.P. Dutton and Company, 1975.

Lagerlog, Selma and Taylor, P. B. <u>The Miracles of Antichrist.</u> Kessinger Publishing, 2004.

Lang, Gerhard. <u>Ophthalmology: A Pocket Textbook Atlas, 2nd Edition.</u> New York, NY: Thieme Medical Publishers, Inc., 2007.

Leeming, David. <u>Oxford Companion to World Mythology.</u> New York, NY: Oxford University Press, 2009.

Lebling, Robert. <u>Legends of the Fire Spirits: Jinn and Genies from Arabia to Zanzibar.</u> Berkley, CA: Counterpoint Press, 2001.

Lecouteux, Claude. <u>The Secret History of Vampires.</u> Rochester, VT: Inner Traditions Press, 1999.

Malpezzi, Frances M. & Clements, William M. <u>Italian-American Folklore (American Folklore Series).</u> Des Moines, IA: August House Publishing, 2005.

Matthews, John & Matthews, Caitlin. <u>The Element Encyclopedia of Magical Creatures: The Ultimate A-Z of Fantastic Beings from Myth and Magic.</u> New York, NY: Sterling Publishing, 2005.

Perez, Soledad & Hudson, Wilson Mathis. <u>The Healer of Los Olmas and Other Mexican Lore.</u> Dallas, TX: Southern Methodist University Press, 1984.

Radin, Paul. <u>The Trickster: A Study in American Indian Mythology.</u> New York, NY: Shocken Books, 1987.

Redfern, Nick. <u>Contactees.</u> Pompton Plains, NJ: New Page Books, 2009.

Redfern, Nick. <u>The Real Men In Black.</u> Pompton Plains, NJ: New Page Books, 2011.

Rose, Carol. <u>Spirits, Fairies, Leprechauns and Goblins: An Encyclopedia.</u> New York, NY: W.W. Norton & Company, 1998.

Ross, Catrien. <u>Supernatural and Mysterious Japan.</u> Tokyo, Japan:

Tuttle Publishing, 1996.

Shahi, Surendra Bahadur, Ratsh, Christian & Muller-Ebeling, Claudia. Shamanism and Tantra in the Himalayas. Rochester, VT: Inner Traditions Press, 2002.

Spalton, David J., Hitchings, Roger A. & Hunter, Paul. Atlas of Clinical Ophthalmology, Third Edition. Philadelphia, PA: Mosby/Elsevier Health Sciences, 2004.

Steiger, Brad. Real Aliens, Space Beings, and Creatures from Other Worlds. Canton, MI: Visible Ink Press, 2011.

Steiger, Brad. Real Vampires, Night Stalkers, and Creatures from the Darkside. Canton, MI: Visible Ink Press, 2009.

Strieber, Whitley. Communion: A True Story. New York, NY: Beech Tree Books, 1987.

Summers, Montague. The Malleus Maleficarum of Kramer and Sprenger. Mineola, NY: Dover Publications, 1971.

Sumrall, Lester. Demons: The Answer Book. New Kensington, PA: Whitaker House, 2003.

Teiser, Stephen. The Ghost Festival in Medieval China. Princeton, NJ: Princeton University Press, 1996.

Ulmer, Rivka. The Evil Eye in the Bible and Rabbinic Literature. Hoboken, NJ: KTAV Publishing House, 1994.

Von Franz, Marie-Louise & Kennedy, William H. Projection and Re-Collection in Jungian Psychology: Reflections of the Soul (Reality of the Psyche Series). Chicago, IL: Open Court Publishing Company, 1985.

Wendell, Leilah. The Book of Azrael: An Intimate Encounter with the Angel of Death. New Orleans, LA: Westgate Publishing, 1989.

Wentz, W.Y. Evans. The Fairy Faith in Celtic Countries. Buckinghamshire, UK: Colin Smythe Publishing, 1981.

Yeats, William Butler. The Celtic Twilight: Faeire and Folklore. Mineola, NY: Dover Publications, 2011.

Yeats, William Butler & Kiely, Benedict. Fairy & Folk Tales of Ireland. New York, NY: Scribner Press, 1998.

Young-Eisendrath, Polly & Dawson, Terrance. <u>The Cambridge Companion to Jung.</u> Cambridge, UK: Cambridge University Press, 1977.

.

About The Author

David Weatherly is a renaissance man of the strange and supernatural. He has traveled the world in pursuit of ghosts, cryptids, UFOs, magic, and more. From the specters of dusty castles, to remote, haunted islands, from ancient sites, to modern mysteries, he has journeyed to the most unusual places on the globe seeking the unknown.

David became fascinated with the paranormal at a young age. Ghost stories and accounts of weird creatures and UFOs led him to discover many of his early influences. Writers such as John Keel, Jacques Vallee, Hans Holzer, and others set him on course to spend his life exploring and investigating the unexplained.

Throughout his life, he's also delved into shamanic and magical traditions from around the world, spending time with elders from numerous cultures in Europe, the Americas, Africa and Asia. He has studied with Taoist masters in China, Tibetan Lamas, and other mystics from the far east. He's picked up knowledge from African and Native American tribal elders and sat around fires with shamans from countless other traditions.

Along his path, David has also gathered a lot of arcane knowledge, studying a range of ancient arts from palmistry, the runes, and other obscure forms of divination, to alchemy and magick. He has studied and taught Qigong and Ninjutsu, as well as various energy related arts. David has also studied stage and performance magic.

His shamanic and magical background has given him a unique perspective in his explorations into the unknown, and he continues to write, travel and explore, leaving no stone unturned in his quest for the strange and unusual.

David has investigated, and written about, a diverse range of topics including, Hauntings & Ghosts, Cryptozoology, Ufology, Ancient Mysteries, Shamanism, Magic and Psychic Phenomena.

David is the founder of the independent media and publishing company, Eerie Lights Publishing.

He has been a featured speaker at conferences around the world and has lectured for countless paranormal and spiritual groups.

He is a frequent guest on Coast to Coast AM with George Noory, Spaced Out Radio and other radio programs. David has also appeared on numerous television shows including the Travel Channel's Mysteries of the Outdoors, History Channel's Ancient Aliens, Beyond Belief and other programs. He was also featured in the highly successful series On the Trail of UFOs.

David's books include Strange Intruders, Eerie Companions, the Haunted series, the Wood Knocks series, and the Monsters of America series.

To find David online:

https://eerielights.com

Printed in Great Britain
by Amazon

78253751R00154